David Parker

'Discerning the Obedience of Faith'

World of Theology Series

Published by the Theological Commission of the World Evangelical Alliance

Volume 3

Vol 1	Thomas K. Johnson: The First Step in Missions Training: How our Neighbors are Wrestling with God's General Revelation
Vol 2	Thomas K. Johnson: Christian Ethics in Secular Cultures
Vol 3	David Parker: Discerning the Obedience of Faith: A Short History of the World Evangelical Alliance Theological Commission
Vol 4	Thomas Schirrmacher (Ed.): William Carey: Theologian – Linguist – Social Reformer
Vol 5	Thomas Schirrmacher: Advocate of Love – Martin Bucer as Theologian and Pastor
Vol 6	Thomas Schirrmacher: Culture of Shame / Culture of Guilt
Vol 7	Thomas Schirrmacher: The Koran and the Bible
Vol 8	Thomas Schirrmacher (Ed.): The Humanisation of Slavery in the Old Testament
Vol 9	Jim Harries: New Foundations for Appreciating Africa: Beyond Religious and Secular Deceptions
Vol 10	Thomas Schirrmacher: Missio Dei – God's Missional Nature
Vol 11	Thomas Schirrmacher: Biblical Foundations for 21st Century World Mission

David Parker

'Discerning the Obedience of Faith'

A Short History of the World Evangelical Alliance Theological Commission

WIPF & STOCK · Eugene, Oregon

Wipf and Stock Publishers
199 W 8th Ave, Suite 3
Eugene, OR 97401

'Discerning the Obedience of Faith'
A Short History of the World Evangelical Alliance Theological Commission
By Parker, David
Copyright©2014 Verlag für Kultur und Wissenschaft
ISBN 13: 978-1-5326-5490-9
Publication date 4/4/2018
Previously published by Verlag für Kultur und Wissenschaft, 2014

Contents

Preface 9
    Preface for 2nd Edition 10

Abbreviations 11

Chapter I Confirming and Defending the Gospel 13
    Background 13
    Formation 15
    London 1975 16
    Consultations 19
    Third World Theologians 22
    Task Forces, Study Units and publications 23
    Periodicals 25
    Theological Education 25

Chapter II Creating a Space for Theology 27
    Climax of the first decade 27
    Wheaton '83 28
    End of an era 29
    Singapore 1986 32
    Bruce Nicholls' achievement and legacy 34
    Discerning the Obedience of Faith 36

Chapter III A Servant and Prophetic Voice 37
    New leadership – Sunand Sumithra 37
    TC and ICAA 38
    Study program advances 40
    Consultations and contacts 43
    The vision fades 45

Chapter IV Reaching for the World 51
    Bong Ro called in 51
    'Theological Issues of the 90s' 52
    Study Units, Electronic Networking and Scholarships 53
    Korean base for the TC 55
    The fire 56
    Study Units at work 56
    Changes and challenges 57
    TC goes 'Down Under' 58

ICAA..59
'The Uniqueness of Christ' 61
Ethics and environment 63

Chapter V Serving the Church...65
Change of focus 65
Publications and consultations 67
TC at twenty years 69
Pace slackens 71
New focus at Prague 73
'Faith and Hope for the Future' 74

Chapter VI Networking Theologians 79
Revisioning at Pasadena 1996 79
Abbotsford 1997 80
Tuebingen 1998 81
New director...83
Wide ranging projects..84
Consolidation and vision at Vancouver 2000................................86
Ecclesiology at Kuala Lumpur 2001...88
Director concludes...89

Chapter VII A New Role for a New Century 91
Regrouping amidst setbacks 91
Global perspective in Germany 2002...93
Moving on 93
Expansion in 2003 95
Thirty years...97

Chapter VIII Reaching the Goal 2005-09 101
Renewed hopes in 2005...101
Seoul Korea 2005 102
Theological conferences 103
Kenya 2006 104
TWG and other conferences...105
Philadelphia 2007 106
Lausanne Theological Working Group.......................................109
Productive program 110
Bangkok 2008...110
Publications 112
Change in leadership...114
Sao Paulo, Brazil 2009...115

Chairman's resignation..117

Chapter IX Re-Building – An Integrated Unit 2010-2014...........................**119**
    Restoration and new leadership..119
    TC at Cape Town 2010 121
    Executive Director appointed..122
    Progress for the new-look TC 123
    Forty Years of Witness 127

Appendices..**129**

Appendix A **129**
    Vision Statement 129

Appendix B..**131**
    Theological Commission Fact Sheet 131
    TC Publications...134

Photos..**139**

Index..**151**

Preface

At first I resisted the suggestion when it was made by Dr Bruce Nicholls that a history of the Theological Commission should be written, and that I should be the author. Although I have been involved with the TC for nearly twenty years, and in recent years have been editor of our journal and newsletter, I did not think that I was a good choice for this task. However, events in recent years made me realise how important it was to have a clear picture of development and work of this organisation in all its dynamism and complexity. So I have gone about this task with increasing interest and purpose.

I am indebted to those who have already written on the topic, especially Bruce Nicholls as the founder, and David Howard, former General Director of the WEF, and to those who have been willing to respond to my requests for information and help – especially in tracking down documents scattered around the world, and in some cases, poring through these papers. I would like to mention especially Mr John E. Langlois (Guernsey), Dr Charles Weber (Wheaton College), Mr Bob Schuster (Billy Graham Center Archives, Wheaton), my good friend Koh Chong Hor (Singapore) and Amanda Darlack, Assistant to Dr Peter Kuzmič at Gordon-Conwell Theological Seminary. An earlier version of this history was published in three parts in *Evangelical Review of Theology* Volume 28 (2004).

The main sources for this history are, of course, the official records of the WEF/A Theological Commission, including minutes, correspondence, reports and publications, many of which are now lodged with the Billy Graham Center Archives, Wheaton, Illinois, USA. My deep appreciation is also offered for additional information supplied by the following: J. Allan, R. E. Bell, R.W. Ferris, K. Gnanakan, R. Kemp, P. Kuzmič, J. Mudditt, C. Sugden, T. Zaretsky, and the WEA International Office. I am particularly thankful for those former leaders who contributed to the special 30th anniversary features that were published in *Evangelical Review of Theology* and *Theological News* during 2004.

The more I have delved into the story, the more I appreciate the contributions made by the vast range of people who have been part of it. It has been a privilege to share fellowship in 'discerning the obedience of faith' with such an honoured band. It is my prayer that this book will enable many others to catch the vision of networking theologians around the world for the sake of the Kingdom.

David Parker, Brisbane, Australia, 2005

Preface for 2nd Edition

Much has happened with the TC since the first edition of this book, so as the organisation reaches its 40th year of ministry, an update is overdue. Although I am no longer involved with TC in the way that I was earlier, I am still pleased to have a part in its life, and especially to produce this enlarged version. There are two additional chapters and the Appendices have been updated.

David Parker, Brisbane, Australia, 2014

Abbreviations

AABC	Accrediting Association of Bible Colleges (now Association for Biblical Higher Education – ABHE)
ACTEA	Accrediting Council for Theological Education in Africa
AETAL	The Evangelical Association for Theological Education in Latin America
AGST	Asia Graduate School of Theology
ATA	Asia Theological Association
BMMF	Bible and Medical Missionary Fellowship (now InterServe)
CRESR	Consultation on the Relationship between Evangelism and Social Responsibility
CWC	WEF/A Commission on Women's Concerns
ELCW	Evangelical Lutheran Church in Wuerttemberg
ERT	*Evangelical Review of Theology*
FEET	Fellowship of European Evangelical Theologians
GA	General Assembly of the World Evangelical Fellowship/Alliance
GCOWE	Global Consultation on World Evangelization
ICAA	International Council of Accrediting Agencies for Evangelical Theological Education (now ICETE)
ICETE	International Council for Evangelical Theological Education (pronounced *eye-set*) (formerly ICAA)
ILT	International Leadership Team of the World Evangelical Alliance
INFEMIT	The International Fellowship of Evangelical Mission Theologians
KETS	Korea Evangelical Theological Society
LCWE/TWG	Lausanne Committee for World Evangelization Theology Working Group
NEF	National Evangelical Fellowship
OC	Overseas Council for Theological Education
OCMS	Oxford Centre for Mission Studies
OM	Operation Mobilisation
SPCK	Society for the Propagation of Christian Knowledge
STL	Send the Light (formerly the literature distribution division of OM)
TAP	Theological Assistance Programme
TEE	Theological Education by Extension
TET	*Theological Education Today*
TN	*WEF/WEA Theological News*
TRACI	Theological Research and Communication Institute
TRL CD	World Evangelical Alliance Theological Resources Library CD
WEF/A	World Evangelical Fellowship, known since 1 Jan 2002 as World Evangelical Alliance
WCC	World Council of Churches

Chapter 1 Confirming and Defending the Gospel

Background

The origins of the Theological Commission (TC) go back to May 1968 when the World Evangelical Fellowship (WEF) (now World Evangelical Alliance) General Council met in Lausanne Switzerland. A key item of business was the resolution of differing views of the authority of Scripture. The use of the word 'infallibility' in the statement of faith adopted by the WEF at its formation in 1951 was perceived by some Europeans to imply a 'dictation' theory of inspiration although this was not intended by those who framed the statement. It was agreed at this 1968 meeting that the position of the European Evangelical Alliance on Scripture was not at variance with the WEF statement, which opened the way for European evangelicals to join the movement. Appropriately, it was decided to appoint a Theological Commission to review and suggest necessary changes in the Confession of Faith for action at the next General Council.[1]

At the same meeting, Bruce Nicholls, a missionary from New Zealand teaching since 1955 at Union Biblical Seminary in Yeotmal, India under BMMF[2] gave a paper titled, 'Theological Confession in the Renewal of Asian Churches.' The invitation had come from the WEF General Secretary, Dennis Clark with whom Nicholls was acquainted through his work in the Indian subcontinent. In his impressive address, Nicholls dealt with critical issues in the theological scene in Asia, such as the state of the unevangelised, inter-religious dialogue, the indigenisation of the gospel and the secularization of society. As a result, he was appointed Theological Coordinator for WEF. Up to this point, Commissions played only a nominal part in WEF work, but the Theological Commission would change that.[3]

After returning to India from his post-graduate research in London, Bruce Nicholls began work immediately by establishing a highly success-

---

[1] David Howard, *The Dream that would not Die: the birth and growth of the World Evangelical Fellowship 1846-1986* (Exeter: Paternoster, 1986), p. 158.
[2] Bible and Medical Missionary Fellowship (BMMF) a missionary organisation originating in 1852 and later known as InterServe.
[3] Howard, *Dream*, pp. 32, 157. Four commissions were established at the formation of the WEF in 1951: Evangelism, Missionary, Literature and Christian Action.

ful Theological Assistance Program (TAP), which took advantage of the resurgence in global evangelicalism occurring at the time. The purpose of TAP was, he said:

> to encourage the development of national theological commissions and societies and the development of regional associations, to offer them consultative help through lecture tours, seminars, workshops and consultations. TAP's function was also to strengthen [evangelical] theological education throughout the third world, with scholarships for graduate training of faculty and support for library development. During the next five years TAP became a catalyst in developing Theological Education by Extension (TEE) projects and accrediting associations in Asia, Africa, the Caribbean and in Europe.[4]

On the recommendation of Gilbert Kirby, Principal of London Bible College and former WEF General Secretary, John E. Langlois, a lawyer from the Channel Island of Guernsey who was completing his theological studies at London Bible College, was appointed as administrator and treasurer of TAP. According to Bruce Nicholls, John, who remained with the TC until 1984, was 'God's gift to WEF'. It was a good partnership of a visionary leader and meticulous administrator.

Publications were an important part of TAP's work. The first was the quarterly *Theological News* commenced in May 1969, produced by Nicholls and then assisted by Langlois.[5] Another of the early publications was a quarterly entitled *Programming News*. This was initiated by Langlois to meet a need in the field of Theological Education by Extension (TEE). A great deal of work was being developed at that time in TEE, but not much of a practical nature was available in programming materials. Martin Dainton was the first editor, and a selection of articles was published in 1977 under the title *Introduction to Programming*. In 1976 *Programming News* was expanded and renamed *Theological Education Today*. The editor was Patricia Harrison, an educationalist from Australia with a strong interest in theological education in non-western countries, who in 1974 became the third member of the TC staff in the position of Theological Education Secretary.

Within the first year of TAP's life, several projects had been established or were in planning, including an information service, staff consul-

---

[4] Bruce J. Nicholls, 'The History of the WEF Theological Commission 1969-1986', *Evangelical Review of Theology*, Jan 2002 Vol 26 No 1, p. 7.

[5] *TN* continued to be published by John Langlois until 1985 when Jeremy Mudditt of Paternoster Press published it for the following four years on behalf of the TC.

tative services, regional consultations, evangelical theological societies, consultations, research centres and numerous publications. Nicholls' vision for regional branches of TAP to be developed in all parts of the world came to fruition quickly in Asia.

At the Asia-South Pacific Congress on Evangelism held in Singapore 1968, the need for closer cooperation between evangelical theological institutions was strongly expressed. This led to Dr Saphir Athyal, Vice-Principal of Union Biblical Seminary, Yeotmal, India, undertaking a tour of theological colleges in east Asia. As a result, a meeting of fifty one evangelical leaders took place in Singapore, 5-7 July, 1970, convened by Dr Athyal, representing the concerns of the Asia-South Pacific Congress on Evangelism and Bruce Nicholls, who represented TAP. A commission of nine members was appointed and plans for an advanced centre for theological studies were laid.[6] A further consultation was called for 8-12 June 1971 in Singapore to implement these decisions. At this meeting TAP-Asia was born, Dr Athyal was reappointed General Coordinator and regional and functional coordinators were appointed. Dr Bong Ro became the full time director, a position he held for the next twenty years. TAP-Asia voted to become a member body of TAP-International but maintained its autonomous nature. Three years later it changed its name to the Asia Theological Association.

During this time there was extensive development in evangelical theological education in many parts of Africa, Asia and Latin America especially, with the formation of seminaries and graduate schools and an increase in the level of training amongst faculty. TAP tracked these developments and offered assistance and encouragement wherever it could; it provided international links, especially through the personal endeavours of Nicholls himself and his colleagues, which were invaluable in the entire process. However, as time went on it became evident that regional associations wanted to retain their own identity while remaining loosely affiliated with the world-wide body.

Formation

By early 1970s, WEF, under the leadership of its International Secretary, Clyde Taylor, former missionary to Latin America and leader of evangelicals in North America, was working toward organizing itself better, espe-

---

[6] This ultimately came to fruition in the formation of the Asian Center for Theological Studies (ACTS) in Seoul, Korea (originally to be known as Center for Advanced Theological Studies (CATS).

cially using commissions to do so. A number of commissions had been proposed much earlier[7] but they had not developed, and in any case, theology was not included!

With the success of the TAP under the dynamic leadership of Bruce Nicholls' fertile mind who, it was said, 'plans projects running into hundreds of thousands of dollars', it was clear that the official formation of a Theological Commission was the next step. Therefore, the WEF Executive Committee, which was working towards a more effective organization, voted at Atlanta, Georgia, USA, on 2 July, 1973, to 'authorize the development of the following Commissions: Theology (TAP), Missions, and Communications.'[8]

Then at the Sixth General Assembly held at Château-d'Œx, Switzerland, July 1974, Bruce Nicholls and John Langlois, reported on the progress of TAP since its inception in 1968. Reports were also given by theological associations in Asia (Dr Bong Ro), Africa (Dr Byang Kato), Latin America (Mr Peter Savage), Europe (Mr Daniel Herm), Australasia (Rev. Neville Andersen), and North America (Dr Arthur Climenhaga). Dr John Stott addressed the assembly on the question of regional theological associations, suggesting that a fellowship of theologians should be encouraged nationally and regionally, and that theological education should be critically reconsidered.

Later in the meeting it was decided to establish the 'WEF Theological Association and that its principal programme shall be known as TAP (Theological Assistance Program).' Those named to serve on the commission were Neville Andersen (Australia), Peter Beyerhaus (Germany), Klaus Bockmuehl (Switzerland), Arthur Climenhaga (USA), Zenas Gerig (Jamaica), Daniel Herm (Germany), Byang Kato (Africa), Gordon Landreth and John Stott (England), Philip Teng (Hong Kong), and Paul S. White (Reunion Islands). Bruce Nicholls and John Langlois continued in their staff roles.

London 1975

The first full meeting and theological consultation of the newly formed Theological Commission was held in London, 8-12 September, 1975, at the London Bible College. Papers were given on the themes of 'The Gospel

---

[7] Howard, *Dream*, p. 157. At the 1968 General Council, when Nicholls had been appointed Theological Coordinator, C. Stacey Woods had also been named Youth Coordinator.
[8] Howard, *Dream*, p. 161.

and Culture,' 'The Church and the Nation,' 'Salvation and World Evangelization'; in addition there were numerous seminars on strategies and structures for theological education, research and publications, regional associations, and other related matters. The results of this consultation were published under the title *Defending and Confirming the Gospel* (edited by Bruce J. Nicholls, 1975).

During this meeting it was recommended that an international council for accreditation of theological schools should be formed. It was also decided that the name 'TAP' should be discontinued and its activities incorporated within the 'WEF Theological Commission.' The Commission was to be expanded to include between twenty and thirty members, with an executive committee to manage its affairs. Dr Byang Kato, the Nigerian General Secretary of the Association of Evangelicals of Africa and Madagascar, educated at London Bible College and holding a ThD from Dallas Theological Seminary, was named chairman; sadly, his promising work as a theologian and national leader was cut short by his accidental death in December 1975. He was replaced by Vice-Chairman, Dr Arthur Climenhaga, who, as a minister of the Brethren in Christ Church, had served as a bishop in Zambia and Zimbabwe and was then a prominent leader of his own denomination's educational work in the United States; he had also been executive director of the National Association of Evangelicals in USA. The pattern was for the Executive, made up of six or seven members representing all continents, to meet annually and the full Commission every three years. Bruce Nicholls credited these regular Executive meetings as crucial for the outstanding success of the TC in the years that followed.

Staff were invariably supported financially by missionary bodies or in some other way rather than being employed by the TC so that salaries were not an issue (although sometimes clerical staff were hired). In 1974, Bruce Nicholls moved from Yeotmal to New Delhi as the founding director of the Theological Research and Communication Institute (TRACI) which aimed to assist the Indian church by providing opportunities for advanced study. From this base he continued the work of the TC until his retirement in 1986. During this period he was ably assisted by a succession of secretaries sponsored by BMMF, namely Miss Liz Brattle (Australia), David Muir and Lionel Holmes (UK). They also made valuable contributions in developing the publications of the TC. David Muir initiated a Research Information Bank for the use of theological schools and produced a forty-lesson programmed text book for teaching New Testament Greek.

Other key figures were the convenors of Study Units, who over the years voluntarily provided strategic and valuable contributions to the work of the TC. Their role was to organize and develop the study, consultation and publication program of their particular unit, which included recruiting members of the group and could include fund raising.

One of the most important functions that Nicholls envisaged for the TC was to undergird the entire mission of WEF by providing a means of developing a sound theological basis for its various activities. This was a particularly vital role since the WEF was by its calling a biblically-based movement and committed to the confirmation and defence of the gospel. This view of the TC's critical role was shared by others in the WEF leadership. This meant that the TC was the most important of the Commissions, and Nicholls was intent on ensuring that it fulfilled this role. So he was constantly looking for ways to advance its work, especially establishing consultations or task forces to examine the theology of such fundamental activities as mission, relief and development and evangelisation, and to clarify WEF thinking on particular issues and problems.

For Nicholls, the TC had five main ministries: theological research and reflection, strengthening projects for excellence in theological education, funding and providing the staff for the semi-autonomous International Council of Accrediting Agencies (when it was formed in 1980) and its members, offering consultative services worldwide through the travel of staff and members of the Commission, and sponsoring consultations and a publications program

He was particularly concerned to avoid duplication of work and resources, so cooperation with other bodies already engaged in similar theological work was a high priority. Through constant travel, correspondence and other means of contact, he developed over the years an intimate knowledge of people and organizations around the world, and drew them into the TC circle, either on a long term or an ad hoc basis. In particular, he focused on regional theological associations in Africa, Asia and Latin America, and other WEF constituents.

He also actively sought to work with global evangelical bodies, especially the Lausanne Committee for World Evangelization (LCWE). There was good cooperation at the level of the LCWE Theology Working Group (TWG) whose convenor was Dr John Stott; six of its ten members were also WEF TC members. Consequently, the TC was actively involved in the Gospel and Culture conference (Bermuda, 1978), sponsored by LCWE; the TC and TWG co-sponsored a number of consultations in the 1980s.

The TC believed that this policy of cooperation also included 'theological conversations with organizations with whom we do not have an

Chapter I Confirming and Defending the Gospel

agreed theological basis or goals, for the purpose of securing information, overcoming unnecessary misunderstandings, for better self-understanding ...'. This meant that contacts with the Roman Catholic and Orthodox Churches, and the ecumenical movement were on the agenda, but this was often seen as controversial by some of the WEF constituency. Byang Kato and Bruce Nicholls took an active part as observers at the World Council of Churches General Assembly in Nairobi in 1975 and Nicholls attended several other WCC consultations.

Nicholls and the TC Executive were motivated by the view that the TC had a key role, serving the needs of WEF and the broader evangelical constituency by helping develop a sound theological undergirding. But they also saw that it had another role – a prophetic one, calling on evangelicals to develop their thinking and to grow in faith and understanding to meet the challenges of the day.

Consultations

These twin roles of service and prophetic leadership were fulfilled through a range of activities, although, in line with the architectural dictum of 'form follows function', the TC structures were kept small and flexible. Perhaps the most obvious activities of the TC were various consultations, commencing with the initial 1975 London gathering. In some cases the consultations were jointly sponsored with other groups, especially the Lausanne movement, and in other cases, they were conducted in the name of WEF generally rather than just the TC itself.

'Church and Nationhood'

The second consultation was held in September 1976, on 'Church and Nationhood' at St Chrischona Seminary, near Basel, Switzerland, involving thirty theologians who issued 'The Basel Letter.' This message summarizing the consultation's thinking on the biblical relationship of the church and the nation in the world was circulated widely through WEF channels and elsewhere. The consultation papers were edited by Lionel Holmes and published by the TC as *Church and Nationhood* (1978).

Hoddeson, 1980

As the Theological Commission developed, more consultations were planned and organized, and these had an increasing impact on the evangelical church as a whole. The year 1980 was the most prolific with six consultations held together in March at High Leigh Conference Centre, Hoddesdon, near London. Two of these were jointly sponsored with the LCWE Theological and Education group.

The first was a gathering of Relief and Development agencies and Third World receiving agencies under the leadership of the Theological Commission's Study unit on Ethics and Society and its convenor prominent American social justice activist, Ronald Sider[9] working on 'The Theology of Development in the 1980s.' Then there was 'An International Consultation on Simple Lifestyle', co-sponsored by Lausanne and the TC unit on Ethics and Society. The Study Unit on Theological Education led by Patricia Harrison convened a study of 'The Teaching of Missions in Theological and Church Education'. Bishop David Gitari and Dr Pablo Perez with their Study Unit on Pastoral Ministry focused on the topic 'Preparing Churches for Responsible Witness Under Totalitarian Powers.' Similarly, 'Reaching Muslims' was a topic for another section, led by Bruce Nicholls and Frank Khair Ullah and co-sponsored with LCWE.

Dr Paul Bowers headed up a conference on the accreditation of theological education. At this time, there were five regional theological associations in different parts of the world involved in accreditation of theological schools and generally in the development of their activities. These five agencies met under Bowers' leadership and formed The International Council of Accrediting Agencies (ICAA),[10] operating with 'internal autonomy under sponsorship of the Theological Commission.'[11] NT scholar and missiologist, Dr Paul Bowers, serving in theological education with SIM International in Kenya, was appointed General Secretary. Under his leadership, the ICAA provided a medium of contact for theological educators worldwide, and a means to promote the improvement of theological education through accreditation, sharing of ideas, resources and fellowship. The creation of ICAA fulfilled an early aim of the TC, and it was the agency through which its interests in theological education were channelled until the mid-nineties when it developed into an autonomous body within the WEF family.

---

[9] Ronald Sider, President of Evangelicals for Social Action, Professor of Theology, Holistic Ministry and Public Policy at Eastern Seminary (Philadelphia, USA) and Director of the Sider Center on Ministry and Public Policy at Eastern Seminary/Eastern University, is best known for his classic, *Rich Christians in an Age of Hunger: A Biblical Study* (Inter-Varsity, 1977).

[10] ICAA has been known since 1996 as the International Council for Evangelical Theological Education (ICETE pronounced *eye-set*).

[11] ICAA Constitution, quoted in Howard, *Dream*, p. 163.

One of the most significant of these 1980 gatherings at Hoddeson was the second, the International Consultation on Simple Lifestyle, which drew together eighty-five evangelical leaders from twenty-seven countries. Out of this consultation, which was responding to the 1974 Lausanne Covenant's call to 'develop a simple life-style', came the most complete and biblically grounded statements which have ever appeared in evangelical circles on the topic. The thorough and provocative papers presented at this consultation were edited by Dr Ronald Sider and published under the title *Lifestyle in the Eighties: An Evangelical Commitment to Simple Lifestyle* by Paternoster Press. This was the beginning of a long and productive relationship between the WEF (the TC in particular) and B. Howard Mudditt and his son, Jeremy Mudditt, of Paternoster Press who were impressed the quality of the Hoddeson conferences. Thus the work of the TC and other sections of WEF became part of the distinguished literary contribution this firm made to the renaissance of evangelicalism.

Similarly, the consultation on development dealt vigorously with the theological implications for evangelicals of the problems of development in the modern world and published its results in *Evangelicals and Development: Towards a Theology of Social Change*, edited also by Ronald Sider. A key focus of the conference was the realisation that much evangelical response to poverty had been pragmatic rather than based on a biblical understanding of the Kingdom of God. It also agreed that the goal of Christian involvement in development should be not only the provision of basic human needs but also social change which secures just relationships in societies. Major papers were presented, inter alia, by Vinay Samuel and Chris Sugden, co-workers in relief and development issues in India, who would figure strongly in the future of the TC.

The full Theological Commission also met during this period of consultations, 21-24 March, as did the WEF itself in its seventh General Assembly. The WEF Executive approved the appointment of forty-seven members for the TC. The TC also recommended to WEF that the LCWE Theology and Education group and the TC form an international theological commission, but this proposal did not eventuate. During the General Assembly, the unexpected reaction of some WEF members to the presence of official observers from the Vatican on the program led to one of the TC's most enduring yet controversial projects.[12] This was the Task Force on Roman Catholicism (later becoming the Study Unit on Ecumenical Issues), which was appointed in October 1980, initially under the leadership of Dr Pablo Perez of Mexico. It began meeting from 1984.

---

[12] Howard, *Dream*, pp. 133-5

CRESR 1982

A significant outcome of the 1980 TC meeting was the announcement that a study program would be initiated on evangelism and social responsibility, co-sponsored by the Lausanne Theology and Education Group and the Theological Commission of WEF. Small study groups were established in different cultural situations and the process culminated in an international consultation which was held in Grand Rapids, Michigan, USA, 16-23 June, 1982, known as the Consultation on the Relationship between Evangelism and Social Responsibility (CRESR).

Fifty evangelical leaders from twenty-seven countries met in what was regarded as 'the most ambitious consultation on that topic yet attempted in the evangelical world.' Plans were made to 'allow for legitimate differences of opinion and understanding of the teachings of the Bible in this critical realm' and 'participants represented a broad spectrum of theological perspectives.' As a result, 'New ground was broken and great strides were taken towards defining an evangelical consensus in the area of social responsibility.'

The final statement of the consultation appeared in 1982 as the Grand Rapids Report, *Evangelism and Social Responsibility: an Evangelical Commitment*, edited by John Stott. This was undoubtedly the most comprehensive statement on this topic ever produced by evangelicals. The papers were published in 1985 entitled *In Word and Deed: Evangelism and Social Responsibility*, edited by Bruce Nicholls.

CRESR was another highly significant consultation whose findings would continue to be an important influence on evangelicalism in the following years. Yet by the time it was underway, the TC and other sections of the WEF family were already strongly focusing on another crucial consultation, to be known as 'Wheaton '83', which would also prove to be a major climax and turning point, especially for the TC and its founder.

Third World Theologians

At the same time, there were other gatherings in process which would have significance for themselves, as well as for the TC and those it was serving. The first of these was a meeting of evangelical missions theologians in Thailand, 22-25 March, 1982 which considered non-Christian world views and various christologies arising from the poor and the oppressed with a view to finding effective and faithful ways of proclaiming Christ. This group, which soon developed into a powerful organization known as The International Fellowship of Evangelical Mission Theologians (INFEMIT) linked with the Oxford Centre for Mission Studies,[13] met again in Mexico two years later to discuss the theology of the Holy Spirit.

The other important gathering was a meeting of Third World theologians held in Korea 27 August to 5 September, 1982, co-sponsored by the TC and regional theological associations on the theme of 'Theology and the Bible in Context.' This arose out of contacts made at the 1980 TC meeting and reinforced later at the LCWE consultation held at Pattaya, Thailand. A 1700-word statement, 'The Seoul Declaration'[14] expressed the outcome of the meeting in developing theologies suited to third-world situations.

These two conferences indicated the growing strength of third-world theologians which was one of goals of the TC. *Evangelical Review of Theology* commented,

> The papers in this number mark an historic moment in the development of third world theological reflection. The degree of unity achieved in the midst of incredible diversity and tensions of cultures, mission and ecclesiological heritages, economic and political systems is remarkable. It reflects a common determination to uphold the primacy and authority of Scripture and devotion and obedience to one Saviour and Lord. We may find fault with the wording of the Seoul Declaration, but its central thrust is clear and augurs well for the theological undergirding of the churches which will embrace three-fifths of the world's Christians by the 21st century.'

Task Forces, Study Units and publications

A second major strand in the work of the TC was the system of Study Units and Task Forces which was developed to focus in detail on various topics of concern and importance. Starting from the consultation held at St Chrischona in 1976, the program was put in place with six 'Study and Encounter Units' (as they were first called) under Lionel Holmes as Project Secretary. They covered the fields of Faith and Church, Theology and Culture, Ethics and Society, Pastoral Care, Theological Education; another one, Mission and Evangelism was conducted in cooperation with the LCWE Theology and Education Group. A budget of $20,000 was raised, and each member of the Commission was assigned to one of these groups with the intention that this would be their primary avenue for TC activity. The number, focus and effectiveness of the Units varied over the

---

[13] http://www.ocms.ac.uk/about/infemit.shtml
[14] Published in *ERT* 7:1 (April 1983), along with other papers.

years, with Faith and Church, Ethics and Society and Theological Education being particularly active and productive.

Both the consultation and the study unit programs contributed to the publication activity of the TC in the form of books containing papers from the consultations and specially compiled volumes embodying the work of the units and task forces.

There was an ambitious plan in 1979 to produce a series of textbooks covering the entire range of systematic theology. Each volume would emphasize the biblical foundations, historical developments and interpretation for contemporary cultural situations, using teams of cross-cultural theologians in the preparation of the series. However, this did not eventuate.

The closest project to it was the series developed by the Faith and Church Study Unit. Consultations were held at Cambridge where the paper writers drawn from various parts of the world discussed their prepared manuscripts in an intensive session of a few days, after which the work was revised and edited for publication. The project leadership was initiated by Dr Ulrich Betz, and coordinated by Dr Richard France (London Bible College), but Dr Donald A. Carson (Trinity Evangelical Divinity School, USA) took over at an early point and edited all five volumes in the series. The first of the books was *Biblical Interpretation and the Church*, which appeared in 1984. It was followed by *Church in The Bible and the World* in 1987.

In 1978 a special series of small booklets was initiated under the title, 'Outreach and Identity'; they were edited by Klaus Bockmuehl[15] and published by Paternoster Press of England and InterVarsity Press, USA. Altogether six were produced until 1983, after which the series lay dormant for a decade.[16] Bruce Nicholls' volume on contextualization proved to be highly popular; it circulated very widely and was still in demand more than twenty years later.

---

[15] Klaus Bockmuehl was Professor of Theology at Regent College, Vancouver, and formerly of St Chrischona Bible Seminary, Basel and Chaplain to students at Heidelberg University.

[16] They were No. *1 Karl Barth's Theology of Mission*, Waldron Scott, 1978; No. 2 *The Biblical Doctrine of Regeneration*, Helmut Burkhardt, 1978; No. 3 *Contextualization: A Theology of Gospel and Culture*, Bruce J. Nicholls, 1979; No. 4 *Evangelicals and Social Ethics*, Klaus Bockmuehl, 1979; No. 5 *Pornography: A Christian Critique*, John H. Court, 1980; No. 6 *Theology & the Third World Church*, J. Andrew Kirk, 1983.

Periodicals

The publication ministry was significantly advanced late in 1977 with the appearance of a journal, *Evangelical Review of Theology* (ERT). The original inspiration for it came from John Stott's suggestion at the WEF Assembly in 1974 that a digest of international evangelical theology be published on a regular basis. Launched in October 1977, it contained full length original articles and reprints selected from other publications in six categories of theology and practice, aiming to provide readers with easy access to the best material available without the need to subscribe to a large number of titles themselves. The publication was well received, and was published at first twice yearly by the TC office in India with Bruce Nicholls as the editor. Later, publication (but not editorship) was transferred to Paternoster Press to improve the production reliability and quality, and in 1985 it became a quarterly. *Theological News* as an eight page quarterly (published since May 1969) also continued its valuable role of sharing information from the TC, WEF generally and evangelical theological interests around the world.

Theological Education

The work of the TC in assisting the churches, especially through theological education, was developed on a personal level most strongly by the lecture tours of TC staff and associates. From the earliest days, Bruce Nicholls, John Langlois and other staff were regularly travelling in various parts of the world.

Of all the activities of the TC, the most strategic and influential was its work in developing evangelical theological education globally because of the potential impact of well trained leaders for the church in the seminaries and colleges. The lecture tours fulfilled a useful role as seminaries, colleges and churches in different parts of the world were able to learn from the insights and experiences of others, and to gradually develop a more global perspective on their work.

Another practical step was the creation of a library development fund in 1977 to assist poorly resourced schools in the third world. By this scheme a basic set of theological text and reference books in both English and French would be made available at reduced prices to colleges which needed them. This program continued for many years in assisting schools until they were able to cope better by themselves. Other schemes, such as the Evangelical Literature Trust, sponsored by John Stott, were also active in a very strong way assisting individuals also with grants of books.

Many of the schools were not only poorly resourced with libraries and buildings, but their faculty often possessed minimal academic qualifications. So an important companion scheme was developed to provide scholarship funds to assist faculty members in evangelical schools to gain higher degrees. The first steps were taken in 1979 with the idea of a $100,000 fund to underwrite the scheme, administered through the New Delhi TC office. As a result of an anonymous grant, scholarships to six European, African and Asian scholars were immediately allocated.

The scheme was soon in regular operation. It continued for about for fifteen years before difficulties in raising funds prevented it from continuing. By then, other means of funding higher degrees, especially the John Stott's Langham Trust Scholarship Fund and the scholarship programme of Overseas Council for Theological Education,[17] were available.

A high proportion of TC investment was focused on theological education. This was especially noticeable in terms of the staff which included Patricia Harrison, Secretary for Theological Education, and educationalist, Lois McKinney, who replaced her on a pro-tem basis. Many of the publications, including *ERT*, were intended to assist theological educators, while the pages of *TN* were filled with news of developments from many parts of the world.

Perhaps the most tangible and strategically important of all was the TC's sponsorship of The International Council of Accrediting Agencies (ICAA). Following its establishment in 1980, the ICAA was instrumental in encouraging and strengthening theological education through its conferences, publications and other activities. It eventually covered all continents through its eight member bodies. In September 1982, Dr Robert Youngblood, missionary of the Presbyterian Church of America holding a doctorate in education, was appointed General Secretary. He first joined WEF in 1979 where he was based in Holland as a Project Officer and WEF representative in Europe. As the new ICAA Secretary, he replaced Dr Bowers who had resigned due to the pressure of other duties. Dr Youngblood was reappointed for another three-year term in August 1985, and after his resignation in 1988, was succeeded by Dr Roger Kemp of Australia in 1989.

---

[17] Overseas Council was founded in 1974 to help effective Christian leaders for the non-Western world through strategic partnerships with seminaries and Bible colleges providing assistance for student scholarships, faculty scholarships, campus development, educational resources, and consultation.

Chapter II Creating a Space for Theology

Climax of the first decade

By the time it was reaching its first decade, the record of the TC was good, its program full, and its prospects promising, but 1983, with its busy round of activities, was to be a major turning point. TC membership had been increased to fifty-four members to provide greater global participation; the executive had also been enlarged.

The Study Unit Program was working well, with groups devoted to Faith and Church (Don Carson), Mission and Evangelism, (Patrick Sookhdeo), Ethics and Society (Ron Sider), Pastoral Care (David Gitari) and Theological Education (Robert Youngblood). There were Task Forces on Church and China (Jonathan Chao) and Roman Catholic Theology and Practice (Paul Schrotenboer). A new study unit had been formed on Ecumenical Issues to incorporate the work of the Task Force on Roman Catholicism. The Scholarship program was also working effectively. ERT had made a name for itself and was ready to be increased to quarterly publication in 1985.

Another significant publication was also being prepared for launching. The work of the Ethics and Society Study Unit, led by Ronald Sider, revealed the need for attention in the field of social ethics. Already, there had been some consultations and meetings on the topic, a textbook had been planned and assistance was being given to theological schools in acquiring library holdings in the field. Now, as a result especially of the 1982 conference, CRESR, it was decided that there was need for an 'international journal of Christian Social Ethics' from an evangelical perspective. The first issue appeared in January 1984, with the title *Transformation*. It was edited jointly by Dr Tokunboh Adeyemo (chairman of WEF Executive Council and General Secretary of the Association of Evangelicals of Africa) and from the TC Study Unit, Dr Ronald Sider, and Rev. Vinay Samuel. The editors' aim was to present balanced perspectives on key social and ethical issues facing the church, raising issues, suggesting biblical solutions, and calling Christians to creative action. It was a success from the beginning, but because it was, as the International Director described it, 'creative, progressive and at the same time controversial',[18] it would later become a source of difficulty for the TC.

---

[18] Howard, *Dream*, p. 171.

The ICAA had held its first consultation in 1981 in Malawi focusing on the 'renewal of theological education.' The work of that gathering, published in 1983 as its 'Manifesto on the Renewal of Evangelical Theological Education' (revised in 1990 and again in 2002), has proved to be a creative and effective guide for theological educators ever since. Further consultations were held in 1982 in Seoul, Korea, in 1983 at Wheaton, USA, and in 1984 at Katydata, Cyprus, where the topic was 'Theological Education by Extension', papers from which were published as: *Cyprus: TEE Come of Age* (edited by Robert L. Youngblood).

The TC consultation program was set to continue in May 1985 when it joined forces once again with the Theology Working Group of the Lausanne Committee to conduct a Consultation on the Holy Spirit and Evangelism in Oslo, Norway. Its declaration appeared in *Theological News* and there were reports in *Evangelical Review of Theology*.[19] Dr David Wells (Gordon-Conwell Theological Seminary, Massachusetts) gave his understanding of the proceedings in *God the Evangelist: How the Holy Spirit Works in Bringing Men and Women to Faith,* published by Eerdmans and Paternoster in 1987.

Wheaton '83

The most important event of this period, however, was the complex of consultations known as 'Wheaton '83'. Planning began late in 1980 when the TC Executive Committee met at Amerongen, Holland 24-27 October, 1980, and called for continuing in-depth study at local, national, and continental levels on four critical issues confronting evangelicals. These were: The Understanding and Use of the Bible; The Evangelization of the World's Poor; The Church's Response to Political Power and Religious Persecution; and The Role of Theological Education in the Renewal and Mission of the Church.

It was decided to conduct a study program for each topic leading to a series of international consultations, with other commissions of the WEF invited to share in the process. While this process was initiated by the TC with Bruce Nicholls as the chief coordinator, others groups, including LCWE and World Vision, were also involved.

The consultation met at Wheaton College in June 1983 (hence the name 'Wheaton '83'), with the topic 'The Nature and Mission of the Church', bringing 370 men and women from sixty countries.

---

[19] *TN* Vol 17 No 3 Sept 1985; *ERT* Oct 1985.

There were three tracks. The first, 'The Church in its Local Setting', chaired by Dr Pablo Perez of Mexico, concentrated on how the church in its local setting is to fulfil its role as 'God's primary agent in his mission for the world.' The second, 'The Church in New Frontiers in Missions', was chaired by Patrick Sookhdeo[20] of London and focused on how the church needs to cooperate within itself and with para-church agencies in order to reach the unreached. The final track, 'The Church in Response to Human Need', under the leadership of Dr Tom Sine, had already been planning its own conference independently of WEF, but then saw the value of integrating with 'Wheaton 83'. It spoke with the conviction that 'Christ's followers... are called, in one way or another, not to conform to the values of society but to transform them.' The word 'transformation' became the key word for what had previously been referred to as 'development.'

The results of 'Wheaton '83' were published in a 'Letter to the Churches' representing the consensus of participants' conclusions and in a series of books.

End of an era

This was a landmark event with a strong sense of partnership during the preparations and the conference itself. Well over half the participants came from the Third World, and a joyous spirit of worship, prayer and celebration was evident. The use of case studies gave a strong sense of the importance, diversity and complexity of the church's worldwide nature and mission. This impacted deeply on participants who soon came to see that the local church was God's primary agent for mission in the world.

Of all the people impacted by Wheaton '83, none was more significant than the chief coordinator himself, Bruce Nicholls, who said it was 'the high point of my conference experience.' He was deeply affected by the emphasis of the conference on a closer relationship with the church and in the process, greater accountability of Christian leaders. But it had more than theoretical significance for him – it touched him personally, with the result that he announced soon after that he would leave his theological work and spend the remaining years of his working life in pasto-

---

[20] Patrick Sookhdeo, born in Guyana, South America, of Pakistani-Indian heritage, is director of the Barnabas Fund, and Director of the Institute for the Study of Islam and Christianity, a Christian research institute specialising in the status of Christian minorities in the Muslim world.

ral work within the ministry of the Church of North India. He gave the TC notice that he would conclude in his role with the organization within three years, in 1986.

There were other changes too about this time. In 1984 John Langlois concluded fifteen years of highly significant and sacrificial participation by himself and his wife. He continued his work more widely in the WEF as Honorary Treasurer and member of the WEF International Council, positions to which he was appointed in 1980 and has continued to hold up to the present.[21] Paul Bowers also left the ICAA although he remained in contact as a consultant and continued to be involved actively and behind the scenes up to the present. He was replaced as General Secretary by Robert Youngblood who had been TC Project Secretary. In a new development, Richard Hart of the Programme for Theological Education by Extension in Jordan was appointed in 1985 to foster interest in this aspect of theological education, indicating its growth and the importance ICAA placed in it. Theological Education Secretary, Patricia Harrison, who had gone on study leave in 1981, announced her resignation and concluded by 1983.

The Outreach and Identity series of monographs saw its last issue in 1983 with J. Andrew Kirk's *Theology and the Third World Church*.[22] The series was to be replaced by volumes produced by the various Study Units of the TC, but only the Church and Faith Unit ever contributed.

Another setback for the TC was the fate of the new journal from the Ethics and Society unit, *Transformation*. It was anticipated from the beginning that it could be controversial. As early as June 1985, it was the subject of debate at a meeting of the WEF Executive Council, which conceded that it was fulfilling a vital and necessary function. However, there was strong disagreement over whether it should be associated with the WEF because of the organization's role in fostering unity amongst evangelicals and the potential difficulties of the WEF appearing to endorse views that might be expressed in the journal. Accordingly, it decided (although not unanimously) that 'in view of the nature and purpose of *Transformation*, we strongly recommend that the Theological Commission make arrangements for its continuing publication as an independent journal.'[23]

---

[21] John Langlois also became a key figure in the WEF Religious Liberty Commission. In January 2005 he was awarded the Order of the British Empire (OBE) for his work in WEF as well as for his other extensive contributions to public life.

[22] Dr. J. Andrew Kirk, a member of the TC and of the Latin American Theological Fraternity, served in Argentina for eleven years with the South American Missionary Society.

[23] Howard, *Dream*, p. 172.

Chapter II Creating a Space for Theology

The next triennial meeting of the TC was planned for mid-1986 in association with a consultation and the 8th General Assembly of the WEF in Singapore. This would be Bruce Nicholls' last event as Executive Secretary, and it would also mark the end of the term of the current chair, Dr David Gitari.[24]

In June 1985, the WEF Executive Committee finalised its quest for a replacement for Bruce Nicholls. The post would be filled by two non-westerners. Dr Sunand Sumithra of India would be Associate Executive Secretary from October 1985, and Dr Tite Tiénou from Upper Volta/Burkino Faso, would become Executive Secretary from July 1986. Both positions would be full time.

Dr Sumithra, a former engineer with a D.Theol. from the University of Tuebingen, Germany, had taught at the Union Biblical Seminary in Yeotmal and in Pune from 1972 to 1985. He also had pastoral experience as a minister of the Methodist Church in India. Dr Tiénou, a member of the TC since 1980, had been offered a staff position earlier, to be taken up when he completed his PhD studies at Fuller Theological Seminary; he would share his time with the Association of Evangelicals of Africa and Madagascar (AEAM). However, this plan did not eventuate. At the time of this announcement, he was teaching at Alliance Theological Seminary in Nyack NY.

The appointment of these two men was regarded as an indication of the growing confidence among evangelicals in the coordinating ministries of the Theological Commission at a global level. However, the arrangement would not be realized, and the stability of Bruce Nicholls' eighteen-year leadership of the TC would not be replicated, much to the detriment of the organization and its ministry.

Sunand Sumithra assisted Bruce Nicholls at the New Delhi office from October 1985, taking over from Dr Robert Youngblood who now gave half his time as Assistant General Director of WEF (working under the General Director Dr David Howard), while continuing as ICAA General Secretary.

The main focus for the TC during these busy months, in addition to its regular program, was the preparation of the 1986 TC meeting and Consultation to be held at the National University of Singapore, 27 June – 2 July,

---

[24] David Gitari, a former General Secretary of the Pan-African Fellowship of Evangelical Students, and of the Bible Society of Kenya, was Anglican Bishop of Mt. Kenya East from 1975, and Bishop of Kirinyaga Diocese from 1990; in 1997 he became Archbishop of Kenya, retiring in 2002. Strongly influenced by the Lausanne Congress, he was a leading advocate of holistic witness in Kenya ('Church and Politics' *ERT* 28:3 (July 2004) pp. 220-231). He was chair of the TC 1980-86.

1986. The theme chosen for the Consultation was 'Christ our Liberator and Redeemer', focusing on 'the basic issues of a theology of evangelism, peace and justice, the role of the Church in giving practical leadership in a world of escalating violence and death.' It would 'work towards a biblical and evangelical theology of liberation and redemption' and help participants to 'consider appropriate Christian practice and lifestyle for today's world.'[25]

It was intended, as *TN* reported, that the consultation would 'mark a new dimension in the evangelical understanding and give prophetic leadership to our churches in times of crisis.' In Bruce Nicholls' understanding, the TC sought to listen to its constituency, and also as a prophetic voice, it aimed to lead them forward in the defence and the confirmation of the gospel.

Singapore 1986

During the meeting, plans for the future leadership of the TC took an unexpected turn when it was announced that there were 'practical difficulties' associated with Tiénou taking up the post. The offer to him had been withdrawn by the WEF Executive Council, and instead, Sumithra was appointed to the position, taking over immediately.

Sumithra had gained some good experience of the work in the few months he had been Nicholls' assistant, especially in a trip to Europe in late 1985. Here, as he reported enthusiastically in *TN*, he had observed a session of the TC Task Force led by Dr Paul G. Schrotenboer, visited the WEF European office in Holland, conferred with funding agencies, and lectured at several seminaries in Germany. He came away inspired and convinced about the value of international networking in theological work, and reported: 'We can never have sufficient exchange of information from Christians in different parts of the world; there is so much we can learn from one another. Here the TC has an essential role to play as a bridge building, as a forum for dialogue, and as a service agency.' However, despite this vision, he was to remain in the position for a much shorter period than expected.

Meanwhile, Bruce Nicholls continued to reside for several more years in New Delhi carrying out parish work with the Church of North India, before retiring with his wife, Kathleen, to his homeland of New Zealand in 1992. Through all this time, and up to the present, he has maintained his vital interest and often his active involvement in the work of the TC.

---

[25] *TN* 18:1 Jan 1986.

Chapter II Creating a Space for Theology

Another disturbing development on the agenda of the Singapore meeting was the instruction of the WEF Executive Council for the TC to dissociate itself from the publication of the journal, *Transformation*. After full discussion, the decision was taken to oppose the WEF Executive's wishes 'in the interests of the WEF's worldwide constituency's witness and integrity'. The meeting empowered the TC Executive Committee 'to clarify the issue' with the WEF leadership should it be necessary. For the personnel of the Ethics and Society Study Unit, this incident marked the beginning of their movement away from the Theological Commission and the ultimate collapse of the Unit.

The 'robust discussion' in the business sessions on key issues of the policies and activities of the TC was intensified by the theme of the consultation itself, 'Christ our Liberator and Redeemer.' Liberation theology was still at that time a matter of controversy in evangelical circles, and the presence of a strong contingent from Latin America (where this movement had its origins) and sympathetic supporters ensured that the topic would be treated with fervour. It was a topic that was chosen deliberately because of the seriousness of the world context and it reflected the determination of the outgoing TC leadership to provide the 'prophetic' lead that they believed was an essential element of the TC's charter.

The papers tackled the relevant issues directly with contributions by Rodrigo Tano (Philippines) on Asian theology, Rene Padilla (Argentina) on the new ecclesiology in Latin America associated with the Base Communities, Valdir Steuernagel (Brazil) on hermeneutical issues, David Gitari (Africa), the Holy Spirit; the papers were introduced by Bruce Nicholls' keynote address and a response by Dr Peter Kuzmič.

Although these papers raised a host of questions in the minds of hearers, the small work groups that had been planned to flesh out the major principles developed in the papers and the preceding Bible studies were not able to meet due to pressure of other business. Planned publications never materialised, thus limiting the value of the consultation, which covered ecclesiology, the challenge of liberation theologies to Evangelicals, and theological methodology especially regarding the practical outworking of theology.

Another delicate matter was the presentation by Dr Paul Schrotenboer of the report on the Roman Catholic Church which had arisen from the previous General Assembly in 1980. The report, prepared by a seventeen-member task force set up by the TC on the request of the WEF leadership, had been endorsed at the WEF General Assembly preceding the TC meeting. This action meant that the division within WEF circles over the matter was formally overcome, allowing those who were concerned about the WEF's stance to resume their participation in the life of the organization. The report was also adopted by the TC meeting, and published in *Evangelical Review of Theology* and in booklet form.[26] This meant that the authoritative position of the WEF was widely available to those who were interested in this issue.

However, it was recognized by the TC that there was more to this matter than merely resolving disagreements with the WEF family by producing an agreed statement on the supposed errors and limitations of doctrines of the Roman Catholic Church. So it instructed the TC Executive to set up ways to examine these issue more thoroughly. Meanwhile, there was a development from another direction. When Roman Catholic authorities became aware of the report, they were not altogether impressed by the picture it painted of their Church. After they raised this matter with WEF personnel, meetings were set up to try to clarify the situation, which eventually developed into a longer series of conversations, expertly led until 1998 by Dr Schrotenboer, and after his death, by Dr George Vandervelde (Institute of Christian Studies, Toronto, Canada).

The 1986 TC meeting appointed Dr Peter Kuzmič as the new chairman to replace Bishop (now Dr) David Gitari whose term had expired. Kuzmič, who was to serve for ten years, was already a TC Executive Committee member, and the founder of the Evangelical Theological Seminary in Osijek, Croatia. Later, in 1993, he took up a professorship at Gordon-Conwell Seminary, USA. A native of Slovenia and a citizen of Croatia in former Yugoslavia, he was regarded as the foremost evangelical scholar in Eastern Europe and an authority on the subject of Christian response to Marxism and on Christian ministry in post-Communist contexts.

Bishop Michael Nazir-Ali (Pakistan), who had also served on the Executive, was appointed Vice-Chairman. New members were Pastor R. Daidanso (Chad), Dr Donald Carson (USA) and Dr Rolf Hille (Germany). A new slate of members was also appointed, forty-one in all were named at the meetings, leaving seven vacancies to be filled later.

Bruce Nicholls' achievement and legacy

As Bruce Nicholls concluded his official work with the TC after eighteen years, he could look back upon a remarkable achievement. Reviewing the past, he said,

---

[26] ERT 10:4 (1986) pp. 342–364; 11:1 (1987) pp. 78–94. Paul G. Schrotenboer (ed.), *Roman Catholicism: A Contemporary Evangelical Perspective*, (Grand Rapids: Baker, 1988).

When I became the theological coordinator of the World Evangelical Fellowship following the Fifth General Assembly in Lausanne in 1968, little did I realise how important the era of the 70s and 80s would be for evangelical Christianity. In the 1960s there were few evangelical third world theologians and educators with post-graduate training in the theological disciplines, few institutions that trained beyond the undergraduate level, and quality theological reflection and writing was sparse. Now the situation has radically changed; no one person or movement can claim credit for it – it is the work of God in response to the willingness for evangelical partnership. But I believe it would be fair to say that the WEF Theological Commission has had a major role as a catalyst in evangelical cooperation in the areas of theological reflection and training worldwide.[27]

The 1986 Consultation would be a culmination of this process for Nicholls, who had been awarded an honorary DD degree from Ashland Theological Seminary, Ohio, USA in 1982. The legacy that he passed on to his successors was a TC that had strongly developed its main ministries of theological research and reflection through consultations and publications, and had strengthened evangelical theological education especially through accreditation, scholarships and lecture tours. As Dr Nicholls saw it, the TC had many roles but above all else, he said,

> It provides an open space where theologians and educators can meet. It is a catalyst for new ideas and projects. Where necessary it coordinates projects on a global level and initiates new ones. The Commission is careful not to overshadow the work of national and regional bodies and is sensitive to their autonomy and self-image. The Commission was not born out of a desire to oppose other bodies, but to encourage and help evangelical theologians and educators to more effectively fulfil the programs and projects they have set for themselves.[28]

Theological Education had been a prime part of the TC work, and would remain so for a few more years still. Bruce Nicholls could fairly claim:

> We have been a catalyst and in some cases a pioneer in extension education, in developing accrediting associations, in library development, curriculum development and scholarships for faculty training. However, theological education is more that building institutions. It begins with good theology which is biblically grounded, contextually relevant and pastorally orientated. Theological education is more than teaching subjects; it is

---

[27] TN 18:2 April-June 1986.
[28] TN 17:4 Oct-Dec 1985.

shaping men and women to know God and to go out to make him known in the world. Men and women need to be trained to be good counsellors, to have a missiological vision and to be accountable to their sponsors. There can be no dichotomy between theological conviction and ministerial formation. Spiritual formation is fundamental to theological excellence.[29]

Discerning the Obedience of Faith

At the conclusion of the Singapore consultation, he handed the work over to his former assistant, Dr Sumithra, who was faced with the task of taking the Theological Commission on to its next phase of development. Sumithra adopted as his goals the principles that had been 'masterfully summarised' earlier by the founder – 'the prophetic ministry of leading evangelicals around the world in current theological debate, and also a servant ministry to meet the needs of the churches, national fellowships, and evangelicals in general.'

In view of this twofold aim and the needs of the times, the new Executive Secretary announced that the TC had adopted as its motto, 'discerning the obedience of faith.' As he emphasized, 'Christian ministries of any type, anywhere in the world must start – not just with action or reflection – but with faith itself.'[30]

---

[29] Nicholls, 'History', p. 21.
[30] *TN* 19:1-2 Jan-June 1987.

Chapter III A Servant and Prophetic Voice

New leadership – Sunand Sumithra

As Sunand Sumithra stepped into his new unexpected role as the sole Executive Secretary of the Theological Commission, he had first to set up his office. This involved moving records and documents from Holland and New Delhi to Bangalore where he lived, first to his home and then later to a separate office, where he had some clerical assistance, including that of his wife. There were also the formalities associated with registering the TC in India, although it was hoped that some of the financial aspects would be handled ultimately through the WEF International office which within a year moved to Singapore.

Taking over the administrative leadership of the TC after the long period of development by its founder, Bruce Nicholls, was a big enough task in itself, without the additional problems of merging and relocation of operations – Nicholls and Sumithra were very different personalities and had different background experiences. Furthermore, as Sumithra himself knew only too well, his strengths were in teaching and theological reflection, not administration, international travel and networking within global evangelicalism. However, his few months working alongside his predecessor had given him valuable insights into the work and strengthened his vision for its value and importance.

So he set about his new responsibilities with determination and enthusiasm, strongly supported by his friends and colleagues in the WEF constituency, and especially the WEF International Director, David Howard who took an active personal interest in his activities. But due to many factors beyond his control, such as poor phone communication, problems of interference with mail and bouts of health problems for Sumithra and his family, it was virtually two years before the administration settled down and he felt that the work was ready to flourish.

One of his most obvious tasks was the preparation of *Evangelical Review of Theology* (ERT), now as sole editor. He changed its format to focus on a particular theme in each quarterly issue, covering a range of topics such as the nature of the theological task, evangelicalism, contextualisation, materialism, and the mission and relevance of the church. Similarly, he was now also sole editor of *Theological News* (TN), which needed to keep track of a wide range of developments in the third world – seminaries, accreditation, conferences, books and church movements – with both reports and editorial comment. There was also *Theological Education Today* (*TET*), printed as a supplement to *TN* and containing usually just one article; it was edited for the first year by Robert Youngblood for the ICAA.

The journals were all published by Jeremy Muddett of Paternoster Press. However, a major part of the responsibility fell to John Allan, part-time Secretary of Publications for the WEF. He was appointed after the adoption of new policies for WEF publications in 1985, and was based at the Exeter office of Paternoster, where he produced a number of books in an remarkably short period. He had to work within a complex framework of relationships. Furthermore, due to distance and poor communications with Bangalore, and other factors, it was always a difficult task to collect relevant material, put it into a form suitable for publishing and keep up with deadlines. He also had to deal with the steady stream of book manuscripts and other publishing projects that were coming in for the TC and other Commissions.

Other prominent TC activities during this triennium were the Scholarship Fund which assisted many faculty members, and the Biblical Library Fund, helping seminaries and colleges by providing books at much reduced prices. These also fell to Sumithra despite plans to transfer them to the ICAA.

TC and ICAA

Theological education continued to be a vital part of the TC's interests. At the 1986 meeting, Rolf Hille of Germany took over as convenor of the TC Theological Education Study Unit, which had previously been led by TC staff workers, commencing with Miss Patricia Harrison, and most recently by Robert Youngblood. Hille, who would later figure very prominently in the TC work, adopted a policy of close cooperation with ICAA to avoid unnecessary duplication. The ICAA itself was now led by Robert Youngblood. In July 1986 he had concluded his part-time assignment assisting in the organization of the WEF General Assembly, and moved to Sequin, Washington, USA, where he set up the ICAA office as full time General Secretary.

During the following months, work progressed on developing ICAA's system of recognition of accreditation services, and the encouragement of accreditation work in Latin America. Papers from consultations were published,[31] and a consultation was held at Unter Weissach, Germany, 23-

---

[31] ICETE publications form a series called *Evangelical Theological Education Today*: *Evangelical Theological Education Today: An International Perspective*, Paul Bowers,

Chapter III A Servant and Prophetic Voice

27 June, 1987, to focus on the renewal of theological education through accreditation.

But all of this positive work was overshadowed by ongoing tension over the relationship of the ICAA to the TC and, more generally, to the WEF. At its 1986 meeting, the TC had suspended ICAA's participation in the TC budget pending clarification of relationships between the two bodies. ICAA believed this issue had been resolved earlier and therefore regarded the TC's unexpected action as a serious problem. This episode raised the question of the precise meaning of the clause in ICAA constitution stating that it 'operates with internal autonomy under the sponsorship' of the TC. It also raised wider issues of accountability in the WEF movement and its organizational framework. This resulted in a strong push over a lengthy period to make the ICAA genuinely an 'affiliate' of WEF (as WEF literature at the time officially classed it), thus making it a parallel organization to the TC, rather than one that operated under the authority of the TC.

On the other hand, some in WEF wanted to reform ICAA to limit its role to a Board of Accreditation, and to assign all other theological education functions to the TC through its Theological Education Unit. However, others, including the ICAA, said such a proposal seriously misunderstood the nature of accreditation which was not a regulatory system, but 'a true catalyst for renewal' touching all areas of theological education.[32] It was also argued that this wider role for ICAA as a full service agency for theological education was part of the original vision when it was established in 1980. This tension over relationships between the ICAA, the TC and WEF was not fully dealt with until the end of the triennium in 1989, but at least at its next meeting in 1987, the TC Executive reversed its de-

---

ed. (1st ed. 1982; 2nd ed. 1994); *Evangelical Theological Education Today: Agenda for Renewal*, Paul Bowers, ed. (1982); *Reader in Theological Education* Robert Youngblood, ed. (1983); *TEE Come of Age*, Robert Youngblood, ed. (1986); *Excellence and Renewal in Theological Education*, Robert Youngblood, ed. (1989); *Text and Context in Theological Education*, Roger Kemp, ed. (1994).

[32] Tite Tiénou, 'The Future of ICAA', *ERT* 14:1 (Jan 1990), pp. 86-91, in which he called for the movement to 'recover and expand [its] original vision.'; ICAA, 'Manifesto on the Renewal of Evangelical Theological Education', *ERT*, 8:1 (Apr 1984), pp. 136-143 (later revised in 1990 and 2002); Robert W. Ferris, *Renewal in Theological Education: strategies for change* (Wheaton: Billy Graham Center, 1990); for B. J. Nicholls' views on global theological education see his 'Theological Education and Evangelization' in J. D. Douglas, (Ed.), *Let the Earth Hear His Voice: International Congress on World Evangelization, Lausanne, Switzerland Official Reference Volume* (Minneapolis, Minn.: World Wide Publications, 1975), pp. 634-645.

cision on the original 1986 motion to suspend financial support for the ICAA.

The first Executive Committee meeting in Sumithra's term was held 31 March – 2 April, 1987 at Korntal, Germany. Despite the administrative and logistical difficulties Sumithra had experienced so far, he approached this meeting positively, calling in his report for the TC (which, he reminded members had both a servant and prophetic function), to focus on key theological issues, better communication and to relate more closely to local church ministry. But it was still a difficult time for him as he continued to come to grips with the extent and nature of the work and his responsibilities as the Executive Secretary.

The meeting grappled with financial structures and administration which were still in a serious condition. As a result, a delegation consisting of Dr Robert Youngblood (who brought his assistant, Betty Froisland) and the WEF Administrator, Dr David Tan, was sent to Bangalore in May 1987 to assist Sumithra in setting up a new organizational system for the TC office. The TC Executive Committee also dealt with membership issues and reviewed the by-laws to improve the structures and functions of the organization.

Study program advances

One of the most significant actions of this 1987 meeting was to set up a new Task Force to provide an official WEF response to the document, *Baptism, Eucharist and Ministry,* which had been produced by the World Council of Churches (WCC) in 1982. Virtually every denomination in the world was taking up the invitation by the WCC to comment officially on the paper; for some time there had been discussions within WEF circles about making a response also. One of the problems for WEF was that, being an interdenominational para-church body, it did not have an official ecclesiology, and therefore discussion of the topics covered by the WCC document was likely to be difficult and controversial. However, it was finally decided that the issue was of such importance that the WEF should make a contribution to the debate, even though the time left for the preparation of a response before the deadline of mid-1989 was short. So a task force was set up, headed by Dr Paul Schrotenboer who had so successfully led the Task Force which reported at to the 1986 General Assembly on evangelical perspectives on Roman Catholicism. His group, consisting of eight people representing seven countries, worked effectively to produce

Chapter III A Servant and Prophetic Voice

a carefully worded 8000-word statement in time for the WCC's process of review.[33]

The most important of all TC activities continued to be the Study Units and Task Forces, which continued on from the previous period, with some changes. Perhaps the most effective was Faith and Church, led by Dr Donald Carson, which continued its productive activities with a consultation on prayer at Cambridge, UK, 6-10 November 1986 involving twenty-five participants from fifteen countries. Its papers were published in 1990 under the title, *Teach us to Pray*, the third in the series from this unit. Two years later, 3-6 November 1988, it met again in Cambridge with twenty theologians discussing papers on the theme of justification. The papers appeared in 1992 as *Right with God: Justification in the Bible and the World*.[34]

Bishop Michael Nazir-Ali, Anglican Bishop of Raiwind, Pakistan, was appointed in 1986 as the leader of the Ecumenical Issues unit, but due to his removal to the United Kingdom soon after, there had been no activity. This area of work was subsequently included in Dr Paul Schrotenboer's Task Force preparing the response to the WCC report.

Patrick Sookhdeo, who led Theology of Evangelisation prior to 1986, had some projects on Islam to complete, including a Consultation on Islam held at Singapore 24-27 March, 1987 with twenty invited participants. So it was more than a year before the new leader, Dr Ken Gnanakan of India, could take over. Gnanakan had been appointed to the TC in 1983. An evangelist in his own right, he was also well known for his pioneering work in establishing in Bangalore a training institution on holistic principles known as The ACTS Institute, and for his involvement in the Asia Theological Association.[35] He conducted workshops for the Theology of Evangelization Unit in UK, USA, Japan and India during subsequent years focusing on the issues of secularism and other ideologies re-

---

[33] P. G. Schrotenboer, (editor), 'An evangelical response to Baptism, Eucharist and Ministry', *ERT* 13:4 (Oct 1989), pp. 291-313; Paul Schrotenboer (editor), *An Evangelical Response to 'Baptism, Eucharist and Ministry'* (Carlisle: Paternoster, 1992).

[34] D. A Carson, (editor) *Teach us to Pray: Prayer in the Bible and the World* (Exeter/Grand Rapids: Paternoster/Baker, 1990); *Right with God: Justification in the Bible and the World* (Carlisle/Grand Rapids: Paternoster/Baker, 1992).

[35] See the Festschrift in honour of Dr K. Gnanakan's retirement, B. Wintle, et al (eds.), *Work, Worship and Witness* (Bangalore: Theological Book Trust, 2003), which includes a bibliography and brief biography. See also W. Harold Fuller, *People of the Mandate* (Grand Rapids/Carlisle: Baker/Paternoster, 1996) pp. 118-121.

lated to the West and world religions.[36] Gnanakan retained his connection with the TC over many years and eventually became Vice-Chairman.

As the result of the response to Rene Padilla's paper[37] at the Singapore consultation on the new ecclesiology in Latin America, an additional Study Unit was named to focus on 'New and Emerging models of the church.' In response to a request for ideas, Guillermo Cook of Costa Rica had submitted the names of several who were interested in the topic with himself as convenor, but these details were not recorded in the original minutes. However, he had proceeded to develop plans for the group to work on the topic at a consultation in June 1988. But when he sought funding, his application was disallowed on the grounds that official sanction had not been obtained previously; however, finances were offered after the event which took place under other auspices.

There was a change in the leadership of the Ethics and Society Study Unit – Dr Ronald Sider's term had expired and he was replaced by Rev. Dr Chris Sugden. While working in India in relief and development work, Sugden had been a partner of Unit member, Rev. Vinay Samuel; he had also been involved in the 1980 Hoddesdon, 1982 CRESR and Wheaton 1983 consultations in this field. He had published some of his own studies[38] and soon became a close partner with Sider in the Ethics and Society Unit.

The Unit continued its record of energetic activity, having met in Kenya in August 1987 and added a new member, Dr Bong Ho Son, who was the founder of the Christian Ethical Practice Movement in his native Korea; he would later become convenor of the Unit. The Unit co-sponsored a consultation on evangelical social activists and charismatics at Pasadena, California, 12-15 January, 1988 where the coordinators were Ronald Sider and Michael Harper.[39] Seminars were held in Korea and the papers from the 1983 Wheaton consultation on the church in response to

---

[36] See *TN* Vol 22 No 4 (Oct-Dec 1991) for a report on the US session, held Sept 1991, and also, Ken Gnanakan, *The Pluralistic Predicament* (Bangalore: Theological Book Trust, 1992), pp. 223-225, notes 1-3.

[37] René Padilla of Argentina was on the staff of the International Fellowship of Evangelical Students (IFES) for many years and was the General Secretary of the Latin American Theological Fraternity from 1984 to 1992. He is President of the Kairos Foundation.

[38] *Social Gospel or No Gospel* (Bramcote: Grove Books, 1975); *A Different Dream – Non-Violence as Practical Politics* (Bramcote: Grove Books, 1976); *Radical Discipleship* (Basingstoke: Marshalls, 1981).

[39] *Transformation* Vol 5 No 4 (Oct-Dec 1988).

human need were published.[40] The Unit continued to publish its journal *Transformation* until mid-1988.

In 17-21 October, 1988 in Hong Kong the Church and State in Asia Consultation which became part of the Ethics and Society Unit, was organized by Dr Jonathan Chao of the China Church Research Centre (now China Ministries International) in Hong Kong in conjunction with Partnership in Mission.

However, the Ethics and Society unit was also the centre of concern over their plans for a visit to South Africa. At the 1986 TC meeting, attention had been drawn to the serious situation of evangelicals in South Africa. Accordingly, members of the Ethics and Society Unit had discussed the possibility of a fact-finding visit there to alert the wider evangelical community to the situation and to provide some encouragement to those in South Africa who had been severely affected by media and communications restrictions imposed by the apartheid regime. Although the Unit had believed their plans had been arranged properly in cooperation with the TC leadership, the report of these developments to the 1987 Executive Committee meeting resulted in serious misunderstandings. It was a sensitive issue for the WEF leadership which interpreted the efforts of the Study Unit as conflicting with WEF processes and related activities. The visit ultimately took place in April 1989 under the auspices of INFEMIT,[41] although the team included some people from the WEF constituency.[42]

Consultations and contacts

The TC was also involved in two important consultations during this period. The first was on conversion which, in continuity with a number of

---

[40] Vinay Samuel and Christopher Sugden (editors), The *Church in Response to Human Need* (Grand Rapids/Oxford; Eerdmans/Regnum Books, 1987). (Previously published as *Selected papers from Wheaton '83, a conference convened by the World Evangelical Fellowship at Wheaton College, Wheaton, Ill., from June 20 to July 1, 1983* (Monrovia, Calif.: MARC, 1983). Arrangements were also made for a Spanish translation. Bruce Nicholls' book on the 1983 Wheaton consultation dealing with the nature and mission of the church had been published earlier under the title, *The Church – God's Agent for Change* (Exeter: Paternoster, 1986).

[41] The International Fellowship of Evangelical Mission Theologians (INFEMIT), formed in 1987.

[42] See report of the visit in *Transformation* Vol 6 No 4 (Oct-Dec 1989), pp. 19-23.

similar efforts previously,[43] was arranged in cooperation with the LCWE Theology Working Group. It attracted about thirty participants from fourteen countries, and was held in Hong Kong 4-8 January, 1988. This consultation was regarded by all concerned as a valuable and highly successful event, and produced a nine-page statement, *The Hong Kong call to Conversion*.[44] The papers were not published, but the main points of the consultation were summarised in *Turning to God: Biblical Conversion in the Modern World*, edited by David Wells, who had done a similar job for the previous consultation on the Holy Spirit and Evangelisation.[45]

Wider contacts were also involved in the second consultation held 26-29 April, 1989 in Willowbank, Bermuda on 'The Gospel and Jewish people.' It was sponsored by the WEF with the unofficial support of LCWE, and chaired by Dr Vernon Grounds of Denver Seminary. The participants included a number of well known theologians and Christian agency heads, including representatives of the WEF and its TC.[46] This consultation arose in response to strong trends in some Jewish and Christian circles towards a view based on the idea of the two covenants – one for Christians and the other for the Jews – that rendered evangelism of the Jews unnecessary and illegitimate. One major denomination was already moving officially towards that view. As a result of the discussions and the skilled work of James I. Packer and Kenneth Kantzer, a 2500-word declaration was adopted and quickly released to the media in time to influence Christian opinion on the matter. This consultation had another outcome – conversations which took place at that time between the TC Executive Secretary and Tuvya Zaretsky, of the Jews for Jesus movement in USA, created the idea of a TC Study Unit on the topic. These ideas were developed and came to fruition at the 1990 TC Executive meeting.

Sumithra travelled extensively as part of his work as TC Executive Secretary. As well as many visits around India, he was in Europe in August 1986 for the Fellowship of European Evangelical Theologians (FEET) conference and then in Singapore to plan for the consultation on conver-

---

[43] They included Gospel and culture 1977; Simple lifestyle, 1980; Nature and mission of the Church, 1983; and Holy Spirit and evangelization, 1985.

[44] *ERT* 16:3 (July 1992), pp. 262–270.

[45] David F. Wells, *Turning to God: Biblical Conversion in the Modern World* (Exeter/Grand Rapids: Paternoster/Baker, 1989).

[46] They included T. Adeyemo, H. Blocher, Bong Ro, and S. Sumithra. Others were Dr Vernon Grounds (Chairman), Dr Tormod Engelsviken, Dr Arthur Glasser, Dr. Robert Godfrey, Mrs Gretchen Gaebelein Hull, Dr Kenneth Kantzer, Rev. Ole Chr. Kvarme, Dr David Lim, Rev. Murdo MacLeod, Dr J. I. Packer, Dr David Wells, and Tuvya Zaretsky.

Chapter III A Servant and Prophetic Voice

sion. He was back in England in November 1986 to participate in the Faith and Church session at Cambridge. The next year, he was in Singapore again for an ATA conference, but plans for a visit to Australia and New Zealand earlier that year failed due to visa problems. He had in mind visits in the future to other countries as well.

Early in 1988 he travelled to USA for the ICAA Executive Committee meetings, joining Dr Rolf Hille in his position as convenor of the Theological Education Study Unit in planning joint activities and in particular, seeking to develop better relations between the two bodies. As well as making good progress in developing ideas for a joint consultation on the theme, 'Renewal and Excellence in Evangelical Theological Education through Biblical Contextualization', the meeting adopted several strong resolutions about the need for reform of the WEF structures as they impacted on the ICAA.

Sumithra took the opportunity while in USA to promote the work of TC. He was not able to visit seminaries as he intended because the WEF North American office did not have adequate contacts in this area, but he did make contact with many WEF donors. He was more successful with theological colleges in the UK leg of this tour, which also included a visit to Paternoster Publications for a rare opportunity of face to face consultation about the publications.

He considered these international travels a vital part of his contribution to the core work of TC – theological reflection and networking; he supplemented these efforts by writing, lecturing and conference participation in various settings. As he reported to the 1988 Executive Commission, this was all giving him a wider and more substantial vision for the Commission: '... more than ever before, I am convinced of the crucial role our Commission has to play in the defence of the Gospel.'

The vision fades

The 1988 Executive Committee meeting was held 15-18 March, 1988 in Bangalore – the first time it had been held in the home city of the TC, although three of the members were not able to attend. Sumithra was able to report positively about the process of reorganization and financial administration, feeling that the worst was behind them. Steps were under way for smoother operation of the Study Units, and the streamlining of administration, by-laws and budgeting. He had made many contacts in his travels and had a better understanding of the global context.

So he was looking forward to the next year or so leading up to general meeting and consultation due at the end of the triennium in 1989. He had gathered many suggestions for topics for theological reflection including the need for pastoral care in relation to family relationships. He was also concerned about 'the need for real theological discernment against the growing influence of various kinds of false teachings' – a topic which would be treated in detail at the next consultation. However, he regretted that the papers from the 1986 consultation on 'Christ the Liberator and Redeemer' had not been published.

The relationship between the TC and ICAA was again on the agenda, with Dr Robert Youngblood in attendance to present his case. Dr Rolf Hille, as convenor of the TC Theological Education unit, also reported. The work of the ICAA was commended, but the TC Executive declined to accept the idea of the ICAA as an autonomous, parallel (or 'affiliate') organization, at least until it could be discussed more fully the following year. However, in a decision that resulted in virtually the same outcome, it was agreed that the work of the TC Study Unit on Theological Education should be related closely to the ICAA and that the two bodies should hold a joint international consultation in 1989 (possibly in Yugoslavia). Soon after, the WEF leadership confirmed that the description of the ICAA's status as 'affiliate' had been an administrative oversight, and that the ICAA General Secretary should continue to report through the TC Executive Secretary to the WEF.

The publication and administration of *Transformation* by the Ethics and Society Unit was also a matter of discussion at Bangalore. At its meeting held soon after, the WEF Executive voted to carry through on its earlier decision that *Transformation* should not appear under the auspices of the WEF. The WEF's audit problems were now stated as an extra reason for this decision. So from mid-1988, *Transformation* passed from the TC to the Oxford Centre of Mission Studies where it has continued to make a vital contribution to evangelical social ethics and mission.

At end of the 1988 TC Executive meeting, the pathway for the future was taking clearer shape – the scene was set for better relationships with the membership and for a more clearly defined Study Unit process and program. Furthermore, uncertainties concerning the Ethics and Society Unit's proposed visit to South Africa were aired and it was endorsed as a low key personal tour for information purposes.

The by-laws were updated and some of the growing administrative problems addressed, but issues related to finances, budgeting and fund raising were still major (and escalating) causes of concern. Some of these were attributable to lack of training, and poor staffing, facilities and communication on the part of the TC, but there were also implications for the overall WEF administration. Although he was aware of these and

Chapter III A Servant and Prophetic Voice

other difficulties, Sumithra himself cherished his experience with the TC, stating that 'my horizons in theological discernment as well as Christian spirituality have been much extended due to my one and half years in this office ... for which I am sincerely grateful to God.'

However, this impetus was short lived, and in a rapid turn of events, the prospects for both the TC and ICAA were soon under a cloud. First of all, in September 1988, Robert Youngblood resigned from the ICAA, one year short of his term, in difficult circumstances at the end of a long period of personal and organizational tension over his role and the status of the ICAA. This meant that the ICAA had to scale back on its joint-consultation plans for June 1989. Even though much planning had been done, it declared that, with reduced staffing, it could stage only a limited mini-consultation restricted to its own members and those of the TC Executive and Theological Education study unit. The involvement of both the TC and ICAA and many from their constituency in the important Lausanne II consultation in Manilla about the same time added pressure for this decision.

In the circumstances, the TC decided to delay its own consultation and general meeting by one year. However, it was agreed that the Executive Committees of both the organizations would still meet in June 1989 as planned, and that there would also be some joint sessions to resolve the problem of their mutual relationships.

Then, when the TC Executive itself met in June 1989, it was presented with the resignation of Dr Sunand Sumithra, even though only a year or so earlier he had spoken positively about his vision for the TC, his personal commitment and how 'the work of the Commission is becoming more exciting to me as the days go by.' Early in 1989, he had presented a detailed and positive report covering the activities of the TC Study Units, and his travel, involvement in conferences, writing and teaching, and ministry and organizational plans for the future. He had been particularly stirred by a conference of evangelicals and ecumenicals on mission, sponsored by the Evangelical Lutheran Church in Wuerttemberg (ELCW) in Stuttgart, Germany that he and other WEF and LCWE people had attended. Discussions there highlighted the great importance of the theological grounding of the church; he came away 'convinced ... that WEF, through its Theological Commission at least, has a vital and unique role in keeping the purity of the gospel in this age of growing secularism and pluralism.'

He was conscious of his struggles with the administrative side of the work, but in the light of his convictions about the value and importance of the TC, he hoped that some solution could be found for this problem, such as reducing the complexity of his role by dividing the theological work from the educational, or securing administrative assistance for him. However, the Executive accepted the resignation, effective September 30, 'with profound regret, recognising his gifts in the areas of teaching and writing, in gratitude to God and deep appreciation of his Christian maturity in all his dealings, and urging him to maintain the closest tie possible with the Theological Commission in the future.'[47]

Although when first appointed, he had not expected to be made responsible for the entire work of the Executive Secretary on his own, he was deeply committed and had made a determined effort to carry out the work to the best of his ability. Considerable physical and logistical limitations of the Bangalore base made his task extremely difficult, and his period in office had been a time of great pressure within the TC because of factors outside his control. He had made a worthwhile contribution on the theological level with his writings, editing and lecturing; even after the conclusion of his duties, he completed editing a Festschrift in honour of his mentor and predecessor, Dr Bruce Nicholls.[48] However, in the latter part of his period of office the pace of TC work had slackened considerably and its administration was in a poor state, leaving the TC Executive Committee and the WEF leadership with the urgent task of making arrangements for a successor to restore it.

Despite these issues, the ICAA mini-consultation focusing on 'Perspectives on the Future' was held in 14-17 June 1989 at Wheaton College, Illinois. During the sessions, Dr Roger Kemp of Australia, a former Baptist missionary who had worked in theological education in Africa, was installed as the new part-time General Secretary of the ICAA.

To resolve the long standing problem of relationships between the TC and the ICAA, the executives of the two bodies agreed on a policy of mutual communication and cooperation, which included sharing in membership of each other's executives. This made them virtually parallel organizations, which is what the ICAA had requested all along. Furthermore, as the convenor of the TC Unit on Theological Education pointed out, this policy meant that his Unit could be dissolved or incorporated into the ICAA. It was decided also that the joint TC/ICAA consul-

---

[47] Dr Sumithra soon found an academic post with post-graduate and research centre, The South Asia Institute of Advanced Christian Studies (SAIACS) in Bangalore, and later engaged in significant research and writing ministries.

[48] *Doing Theology in Context: a Festschrift in honour of Dr Bruce J. Nicholls*, edited by Sunand Sumithra (Bangalore: Theological Book Trust, 1992); an earlier plan for this to be a TC publication did not materialise.

tation planned for 1989 on the theme, *From Text to Context*, would be deferred to 1991.

Chapter IV Reaching for the World

Bong Ro called in

The major issue for the members of TC Executive and the WEF leadership at these meetings was to fill the vacancy left by the resignation of Dr Sunand Sumithra. They appointed ATA General Secretary, Dr Bong Ro, currently on furlough in USA, as interim Executive Secretary on a part-time basis. He would be assisted in some of his work by Dr Paul Schrotenboer.

Ro, a Korean who studied in USA at Wheaton College, Covenant Seminary and Concordia Lutheran Seminary (where he gained a doctorate in church history), originally began working with Overseas Missionary Fellowship at the Discipleship Training Centre, Singapore in 1970. In 1974, he became Executive Secretary of the Asia Theological Association, with his office in Taiwan, where he became extremely well known for his energetic leadership of ATA. He had therefore been intimately associated with the foundations of TC as it emerged from the 'Theological Assistance Program' (TAP) and had worked extensively with Dr Bruce Nicholls, who endorsed his new appointment. Ro was strongly supported by the WEF International Director, Dr David Howard, who continued to take an active part in guiding the TC; Howard and other TC leaders hoped that Ro would take on the position permanently. He was interested in this possibility, but realised he could do so only if there was someone to replace him in the ATA post; he had also another major responsibility – Dean of the ATA's Asia Graduate School of Theology (AGST).

Bong Ro began work by reviewing the Study Units with a view to reviving and expanding them. One immediate issue to deal with was the resignation of Donald A. Carson who had served a lengthy term on the Executive and especially in leading the Faith and Church unit. He stood down from the Executive in 1990, but wanted to continue with the Study Unit until the series of five books was complete.

With so much publishing work to his credit already, Ro needed no persuading that publications were a critical part of the TC program. He was also aware that success would continue to depend on the dedicated and sacrificial contribution of Jeremy Mudditt and Paternoster Press – especially during this transitional period when the practical aspects of their production were extremely difficult to manage. There was increased pressure from mid-1990 when John Allan ceased his role as WEF

Publications Secretary, and was no longer able to bolster ERT and TN as he done before.

To deal with this problem, it was decided to call once more on Dr Bruce Nicholls to take over ERT, the journal which he founded and edited from 1977 to 1986. From his first issue, January 1991, there was a welcome improvement in quality. On the other hand, Bong Ro planned to handle the editing, production and distribution of Theological News himself, changing it into a glossy magazine with many photographs – a style which he had used so successfully over many years with the ATA newsletter. However, it took some time to achieve this. After an embarrassing break of one full year when the newsletter had not been published, the first of the new style issues finally appeared in mid-1990

However, the biggest and most urgent task for Ro was to organize the next TC consultation, postponed from 1989 and now set down for mid-1990 – just a year away. He was well experienced at this type of work and by early in 1990 had confirmed eight paper writers, with plans for others well advanced.

'Theological Issues of the 90s'

The Consultation was held at Wheaton College 18-22 June 1990 with about eighty people from twenty-one countries in attendance. The theme, 'Theological Issues of the 90s', echoed concerns expressed earlier by Dr Sunand Sumithra about the threat posed by the growth of unorthodox theologies and religious movements. Major papers were delivered by theologians from US, Netherlands, India, Germany, Philippines, Romania, Yugoslavia on such topics as the 'New Age' movement, Process Theology, the 'Minjung' theology of Korea, resurrection and religious pluralism, Suffering and Martyrdom, sacrifice and blood in African Theology, the person and work of Christ in Latin America. Reports were given on current developments in theological education in Europe, Africa, the South Pacific, Asia and North America.

The triennial TC general meeting was also scheduled to be held during the Consultation program, but recent changes in the leadership and the associated interruptions to activity impacted this important event. With only sixteen members out of the total number of 42 present, a postal vote was needed to ratify the business conducted. Due to unsettlement in the latter part of the triennium, it was decided that the membership of those appointed in 1986 would be extended to the next meeting planned for 1992.

Executive Committee business could not be completed either due to lack of a quorum. Ward Gasque, New Testament scholar of Canada and Rev. Rev. Pedro Arana (Peru) were nominated as members to replace D.A. Carson and E. Nunez; Bishop Nazir-Ali had also indicated his wish to withdraw. Most important of all, the ATA agreed to release Ro from his position as General Secretary, so the WEF appointed him permanently as TC Executive Secretary, but on a part time basis until a replacement was found for him at the ATA.

Study Units, Electronic Networking and Scholarships

Despite the slow down in TC work during the previous period, the Study Unit convenors gave reports on up to twelve areas that indicated considerable activity – both past and anticipated. In fact, the need was expressed for a manual of procedures so that the many different streams and initiatives could be handled effectively.

Ethics and Society Unit members had been in Korea for lectures, conferences and as WEF observers at the Justice, Peace and Integrity of Creation Conference (March 1990). The conference of charismatic and evangelical social activists in Pasadena January 1988 was followed up in London two years later, giving birth to the 'Spirit and Kingdom' dialogue. A process of studying Christian faith and economics had been established in 1987 and 1990 in Oxford and the attention of the unit would now be given to business ethics, the environment, and issues relative to Eastern Europe.[49]

The Ecumenical Issues Unit, led by Dr Paul Schrotenboer, which had successfully completed two projects during the last decade, was now starting work on the third, an evangelical response to the recent WCC report, 'Toward a Common Expression of the Apostolic Faith.' The report needed to be finalised in 1992 if it was to be included in the WCC review process.

In addition, there had been brief private discussions in 1988 in Jerusalem between the Dr David Howard (International Director) and Dr Schrotenboer for WEF and Roman Catholic representatives about the evangelical statement on the Catholic Church which had been produced in 1986. It was decided that further discussion was needed to understand the issues more satisfactorily. These were set for October 1990 in Budapest involving Dr Schrotenboer (USA) and Dr George Vandervelde (Cana-

---

[49] *Transformation* Vol 5 No 4 (Oct-Dec 1988); Vol 7 No 3 (July 1990); Vol 4 No 3 (July 1987); Vol 7 No 2 (Apr 1990).

da) for the WEF and two representatives of the Vatican. These talks identified some of the key issues, which indicated clearly the need for more extensive study still.

Dr Ken Gnanakan of India, convener of the Theology of Evangelization Unit, reported that a 150-page document had been drafted to encapsulate the findings of its earlier workshops.[50] Two new Task Forces were also set up within this Unit to cover important areas of evangelization – New Age Theology, with Dr Gordon Lewis (Denver Seminary), as convener, and Evangelization of the Jews, a group led by Tuvya Zaretsky, of Jews for Jesus, which had its origin at the Willowbank conference held in Bermuda 26-29 April, 1989 on the Gospel and Jewish people. Zaretsky's organization had made a formal proposal for the Task Force and guaranteed support for its work. The final papers would be presented by May 1991.

During the TC consultation in Wheaton, the participants endorsed the establishment of some additional study projects. A task force on Eastern Europe Needs and Issues would also be established under the leadership of Dr Peter Kuzmič to identify critical theological issues related to new opportunities opening up in Eastern Europe. Similarly, the new world situation called for more attention to be given to non-Christian religions, so initial plans were made for a task force on this topic as well.

Dr Peter Lewis (Pastor of Cornerstone Church, Nottingham, UK) was requested to develop an international initiative on preaching as a result of a report from the Study Unit on Pastoral Ministries. However, there was misunderstanding about the prospects of another proposal – pastoral counselling – because the Director of the Pastoral Counselling Institute had been led to understand his organization could act alone under the TC auspices rather than being part of a more comprehensive Task Force involving participants from outside their own organization as well.

A sign of future trends was also emerged at the Wheaton meetings, when Dr David McKenna, President of Asbury Seminary, with the strong recommendation of Dr David Howard, presented ideas for an electronic network of theologians and seminaries, under the control of the TC and acting as 'an extended Publications Committee.' No action was taken at the meeting, but the idea was promoted on several occasions in later years, especially under the leadership of Dr John Bennett of Overseas Council who was coordinator of a working group on the project. Well before the time of Bennett's premature death in 1999, the TC had found its electronic home on the WEF's website, and the ideas proposed by Dr

---

[50] This manuscript was never published, due to difficulties with the WEF publications process.

McKenna were overtaken by the ready availability of email and e-conferencing.

During the year 1989-90, the Scholarship Fund has distributed $38,000 to seventeen students. At the 1990 meeting, $50,000 was allocated to six Africans and eight Asians, and $30,000 was allocated to Asia Graduate School of Theology and Eastern Europe colleges for scholarship aid. However, signs of change were noticeable when, in response to an approach from the Langham Trust, there was active discussion about cooperation between the two bodies. There was also some discussion of Library Fund matters, but soon after this work was handed to the ICAA.

Plans were also laid for a full scale consultation in conjunction with the WEF General Assembly scheduled for 1992. There had been protracted discussions with the LCWE Theology Working Group to hold a joint consultation, but it had not been possible to reach agreement, so the TC decided to go ahead alone with a consultation on the Uniqueness of Christ and religious pluralism.

Korean base for the TC

Now in his permanent role as Executive Director, Bong Ro concluded his furlough and returned to his homeland of Korea in August 1990, setting up the TC office in the Asian Center for Theological Studies (ACTS). He had already relocated his ATA office to Seoul in May 1990. He would continue to have joint responsibilities for the TC and ATA until February 1991 when the ATA appointed Dr Ken Gnanakan (India) as General Secretary and Dr Rodrigo Tano (Alliance Biblical Seminary, Philippines) as Accreditation Secretary. Ro thus concluded twenty years with the ATA, but retained the position of Dean of AGST.

Ro, assisted strongly by his wife Alma, took up his work with characteristic enthusiasm. As he noted, the challenge he faced was to think globally – not just about Asia. It was a new situation for him and also for the evangelical constituency because he had been so much associated with his famous slogan, 'Train Asians in Asia'. As one who had been immersed in theological education and publications for so long, Ro would also need to expand his thinking about the role of the TC as encompassing more than these functions. However, his efforts at restoring the thrust of the TC were hampered for months by difficulties in setting up his office and securing clerical and other staff to assist him; it was also interrupted by frequent travels and by his other responsibilities.

The early 1990s proved to be one of the most active periods for TC work for years, although political and military events in the Balkans were beginning to impact on Executive Committee chairman, Dr Peter Kuzmič, whose seminary had to be relocated in September 1991 due to the war.

The fire

At the same time as Ro was re-establishing himself in Korea, another event happened far away which would have a continuing impact on the TC and WEF generally. A fire in the new warehouse of Paternoster Publishers on the night of 15-16 August, 1990 destroyed a huge quantity of material, which included the entire stock of WEF publications, not least of which was *ERT* and all the TC books and monographs. The value of WEF material was over $50,000, although that was only a fraction of the total lost by Send the Light (STL), the literature distribution division of Operation Mobilisation (OM) which had moved into the warehouse less than a year earlier and used it as a base for its extensive distribution network for several major UK publishers, including Paternoster. The only surviving WEF materials were those held by Baker Book House in USA, who had begun distributing new WEF books in 1987. Half of the US stock would be shifted back to UK, but it was a major setback, although it did provide an opportunity for the reassessment of the programme of WEF publications.

Study Units at work

Recognising the importance of the Study Unit program of the TC, Ro gave this work a high priority. Faith and Church held its fifth consultation in Tyndale House, Cambridge, UK, 18-20 October, 1990 to finalise its series of books; this one focused on the topic of worship.[51] The previous book on justification was about to be printed, but stocks of the first three had been destroyed in the fire. Dr James I. Packer (Regent College, Vancouver) had been approached as convenor to replace Donald Carson, and had given his informal agreement. But he withdrew in October 1991 before any more projects had been undertaken. This marked the end of a long period of effective work by this study unit.

The newly formed Jewish Evangelism Task Force held its first session 2-5 May, 1991 at Oakbrook, Illinois, with seventeen participants. The Task Force commissioned fourteen papers to be published under the title: 'To the Jew First: The place of Jewish evangelism in the ongoing mission of

---

[51] D. A. Carson (editor), *Worship: Adoration and Action* (Carlisle/Grand Rapids: Paternoster/Baker, 1993).

the church.' However, these publication plans never materialised,[52] and the Task Force did not meet again.

The Ethics and Society Unit was working on plans for a major consultation in association with the Au Sable Institute of Environmental Studies in Michigan, USA for 1992 focusing on the environment, and the ICAA was planning its next consultation for July 1991.

Changes and challenges

However, the strong dynamic that had energised the Ethics and Society Unit from the beginning was now beginning to be focused on other organizations. The impending retirement of Donald Carson from the Church and Faith Unit also signalled the end of a second important plank of TC work. The growing concentration of theological education interests in the ICAA and its consequent development as a viable organization operating in parallel to the TC removed yet another significant element. These three developments, coupled with pressures on the leadership, shortages of finance and uncertain relationships with the WEF, meant that the TC was facing a difficult future.

The AD 2000 movement, a third major world evangelical organization alongside the Lausanne movement and WEF, which began to take shape from the late 1980s was also destined to have an impact on the prospects for the TC and the WEF generally. A conference scheduled for 1994 involved key TC personnel in its theology track, including the TC Chairman, Peter Kuzmič and Executive Secretary, Dr Bong Ro. A report in *Theological News* indicated that Ro saw the new interest as complementary to the TC because it would work at the grass roots level of the churches rather than with theologians and seminaries, but as time passed, this distinction was not so clear.

With the massive changes taking place around this time in the communist world, Eastern Europe was becoming a focus of concern for theologians and theological educators as well as other strands of Christian work. There was even more interest for the TC because of the increasingly prominent role its chairman, Peter Kuzmič, was taking in this area of ministry which affected his homeland so intensely. WEF International Director, David Howard, TC leaders Peter Kuzmič and Bong Ro together with the head of Overseas Council, Charles Spicer, made an extensive tour of six countries in May 1990 to assess the situation, and to introduce the ministries of WEF to evangelical leaders in these countries with the

---

[52] The papers from the Willowbank conference, 1989, were never published either.

possibilities of the formation of their own evangelical alliances. Ro reported on this important trip: 'With such a rapid church growth taking place in every Eastern European country except Albania, leadership training and Christian publications are two most urgently needed ministries. The WEF Theological Commission must pick up the challenge to assist theological education in Eastern Europe.'[53]

On the other hand, there was an opportunity to expand TC and ICAA interests in Latin America with a visit there by ICAA General Secretary Roger Kemp in June 1990. This and later initiatives eventually led to the formation of AETAL (The Evangelical Association for Theological Education in Latin America) in July 1992 with eighty founding members covering thirteen countries in four regions, an additional regional member for ICAA.

TC goes 'Down Under'

The first meeting of the TC Executive after Bong Ro took over the full leadership was held in Canberra, Australia to coincide with the 7th General Assembly of the World Council of Churches, 7-20 February, 1991. The theme of the Assembly, 'Come Holy Spirit, renew the whole creation,' was of interest to many evangelicals, and several were present, some with TC connections. A statement of evangelical concerns was issued at the end of the Assembly and a separate report was presented to the WCC leadership calling for changes to give evangelicals a greater voice. The statement acknowledged that evangelicals were challenged by various themes that emerged in the Assembly, including the call to unity, the needs of indigenous and marginalised people, the role of women, issues of syncretism and for care and skill in dealing with the complex theology of issues related to justice, peace and the integrity of creation. This was the first experience for the TC with a major world event and the ability to make informed comment, especially in the form of a publication two years later which would be a resource for interested members of the evangelical constituency.[54]

The TC Executive meeting, conducted in Canberra 15-16 February, 1991, just prior to the WCC Assembly, was the first (and only one so far) to be held in the southern hemisphere. It was also the first for new members Dr Ward Gasque (North America) and Rev. Pedro Arana (Peru); the

---

[53] *TN* Vol 21 No3 (July 1990), pp. 2-3.
[54] TC officials such as Dr B. J. Nicholls had been in attendance at earlier WCC events, including the 5th Assembly, Nairobi, 1975.

vacancy caused by Bishop Nazir-Ali's withdrawal was filled with an invitation to Emmanuel Gbonigi, Anglican Bishop of Akure, Nigeria. While the financial situation was not serious, Tony Lee, WEF Administration Director and TC Treasurer, was present to give advice, reminding the Executive of the need to keep good control of expenditure, and to seek more funding, especially from North America.

With the next general meeting and consultation only a year away, it was decided to extend once again the term of TC members appointed in 1986 – this time to 1995, and to plan for a wider representation by appointing additional people. Dr Ro was making some progress in his new role, but he had been hampered by delays in relinquishing his ATA responsibilities and in the arrival of office assistance.

Dr Bruce Nicholls, who had begun work again as editor of *ERT* with the January 1991 issue, continued the thematic plan and encouraged convenors of study units to contribute material. Discussion centred on ways to reduce subscription prices and to broaden the circulation base with subsidies for needy institutions, greater publicity, and cheaper printing and postal arrangements outside the UK. It was decided to continue the preparation of the monograph series, which Ro would take up with considerable enthusiasm later.

There had not been much time for more activity from the Study Units since the previous meeting, but plans for various projects were well in hand. However, concerns were expressed about the health of the convenor of Ecumenical Issues, Dr Paul Schrotenboer. The Theology of Evangelization Unit was planning to follow up its earlier workshops with a session at Fuller Seminary in September 1991, focusing on the broader framework of the Kingdom of God in the context of secularism and atheism, while another group would meet in Japan.[55] Dr Peter Kuzmič gave a passionate plea for help which was urgently needed to develop the Task Force on Eastern Europe and to supply teaching faculty, libraries and text books in national languages in response to the new opportunities and pressures for ministry and training in the countries of Eastern Europe.

ICAA

The work of the ICAA was also an important item of business, with General Secretary, Dr Roger Kemp present throughout the meeting. There was considerable discussion once more about relationships between the TC and ICAA. The convenor of the Theological Education Unit, Dr Rolf

---

[55] *TN* Vol 22 No 4 (Oct-Dec 1991), p. 4f.

Hille, and Dr Bong Ro were asked to set up discussions with the ICAA with 'a view to closer identity.' Plans were endorsed for the joint consultation to be held in July 1991 at the London Bible College where the theme would be, 'From Text to Context in Evangelical Theological Education.' The papers from the conference, which proved to be a successful event, including several by TC personnel, such as Donald Carson, Bong Ro and Rolf Hille, were published by the ICAA in 1994.[56] However, it was apparent that the close connection between the TC and the ICAA was starting to dissolve, a process that would continue over next few years, culminating in a major new approach by the latter in 1996.

Another significant development was noted by Bong Ro in a report on a conference he attended in April 1991,[57] which he described as 'somewhat different' from others he had attended. He was referring to the 4th INFEMIT Conference held at Osijek, Yugoslavia which discussed the 'biblical mandate for socio-political concerns of the Christian church and formulated the biblical evangelical theology of social justice and political freedom.' What struck Ro first of all was that conference participants were 'committed evangelicals who believe in the historical-biblical faith of the Christian church with much concern for Christian social responsibility.' He found that the 'discussion widened the scope of evangelism, church ministry and social concerns.' A second point was that, unlike many other conferences where Westerners usually dominated, this one was led mainly by the two-thirds world theologians and church leaders, including in this case Vinay Samuel, Rene Padilla, Samuel Escobar and Kwame Bediako (although Ronald Sider and Chris Sugden were also present) – all of whom had strong links with the Theological Commission.

Such ideas may have been 'somewhat different' for Ro, but they had been on the TC agenda at least since the early 1980s and especially in the establishment of *Transformation* magazine by the Ethics and Society Unit. These views had been vigorously encouraged in the early days of the TC by a previous WEF General Secretary, Waldron Scott, who was noted for his robust belief in the positive relationships between mission, discipleship and social justice. While in the WEF office, he adopted the policy that WEF should function as an 'umbrella' organization, 'providing a place for

---

[56] R. Kemp (editor), *Text and Context in Theological Education*, (ICAA Monograph Series No. 4) (Springwood: ICAA, 1994).

[57] *TN* Vol 22 No 3 (Apr-June 1991); *Transformation* Vol 8 No 3 (July-Sept 1991), pp. 1-6.

Chapter IV Reaching for the World

evangelicals of all persuasions to come together ... in an "open space" without undue restrictions.'[58]

What was true about Ro's observation was the growing influence of such views on social justice in the wider evangelical community and the way some TC members and others were developing their relationships and their ideas on third-world missiology through the INFEMIT organization and allied bodies. This was particularly noticeable in the journal *Transformation* and its associated research institution, the Oxford Centre for Mission Studies.[59] Such developments were not encouraged by the current WEF leadership.

'The Uniqueness of Christ'

The focus of TC interest was increasingly directed to the next consultation and general meeting originally planned for Bogor, a resort centre outside Jakarta in Indonesia in June 1992 as part of the 9th WEF General Assembly. However visa and other problems led to it being transferred at relatively short notice to the Philippines, first at Lake Taal but then, on account of potential volcanic activity in the area, it was moved first to one site in Manila and then finally to the Hyatt Regency Hotel.

Despite all this dislocation, the TC Consultation went smoothly with eighty-five present from twenty-eight countries. Twenty papers were presented in a packed program, focusing sharply on the theme, 'The Unique Christ in our Pluralistic World.'[60] Veteran TC leader, Dr Bruce Nicholls introduced the topic in his keynote address by stressing the importance of understanding the exact meaning of Christ's uniqueness and effectively relating this to all aspects of Christian life and culture. The plenary speakers presented a summary of their papers, covering the uniqueness of Christ in relation to various sub-topics: plurality of reli-

---

[58] David Howard, *The Dream that would not Die: the birth and growth of the World Evangelical Fellowship 1846-1986* (Exeter: Paternoster, 1986), p. 123; Scott, who served at various times with The Navigators, LCWE, American Leprosy Mission and other groups, was General Secretary of WEF, 1975-81; see *Transformation* Vol 8 No 4, 1991 pp. 16-18,22 for his biography and work with Holistic Ministry International, and his *Bring Forth Justice: a Contemporary Perspective on Mission* (Grand Rapids: Eerdmans, 1980); he was also the author of one of the TC monographs, *Karl Barth's Theology of Mission* (1978).

[59] See Dr C. Sugden, 'Mission Leadership and Christian Theological Research' ERT 28:3 (July 2004) pp. 232-246 developments and thinking that led to the formation of INFEMIT and the Oxford Centre for Mission Studies.

[60] The Asia Theological Association shared in this consultation.

gions, the challenge of modernity, diversity and unity of church understandings, political ideologies, the hope and judgement of the world and peace and justice. A 6500-word declaration was produced and ultimately the papers were published, thus making them available to a wider audience.[61]

Reports indicated that ERT was in good condition, although the subscription rate was still considered to be too high. Ro was been discussing with Overseas Council how the Scholarship Program could be extended. Two more consultations were being planned – one on Eschatology with the AD2000 movement (which did not eventuate), and another on Evangelization of the Poor. There were positive reports from the Expository Preaching Unit led by Dr Peter Lewis (UK), Evangelisation (Dr Ken Gnanakan) and Ethics and Society (Dr Chris Sugden). Outside the TC orbit, but involving the efforts of both the chair and the Executive Secretary, there would be the GCOWE II (Global Consultation on World Evangelization), sponsored by the AD2000 movement, in June 1994.[62]

A major item of business was the adoption of the report of the Ecumenical Issues Task Force on the 'Confessing the One Faith' project. The Convenor, Dr Schrotenboer, made recommendations about further studies covering Scripture and Tradition, Evangelism and Salvation in Inter-Church relations and Evangelicals and Visible Unity. The first of these would be the subject of the Unit's next project. He also foreshadowed that the WEF Executive had agreed to further talks with the Roman Catholic Church to address in depth some of the issues arising from the 'Contemporary Evangelical Perspectives on Roman Catholicism' report of 1986. Following up on the introductory sessions held in 1988 and 1990, it was clear that the earlier report had dealt only with the familiar polemic doctrinal differences between evangelicals and Roman Catholics rather than the underlying issues such as Scripture and tradition, and the nature of the Church. These would be the subject of the ensuing talks.

It was reported that the long delayed book of papers on the WCC assembly, *Beyond Canberra: Evangelical Responses to Contemporary Ecumenical Issues*, edited by Nicholls and Ro, had met with the disapproval of the WEF

---

[61] Bruce J. Nicholls (editor), *The Unique Christ in our Pluralist World* Nicholls (Carlisle/Grand Rapids: Paternoster/Baker, 1994). Some of the papers were also published in ERT 17:1 (Jan 1993), which was devoted to the topic of the 'Uniqueness of Christ' and the statement was published as one of the TC 'Outreach and Identity' Series monographs in 1993.

[62] The date was later changed to 17-25 May, 1995.

Executive. It was decided to appeal for a reversal of this decision, but if this failed, then the editors were free to find another publisher.

At the conclusion of the 1992 meeting, over fifty names were proposed as TC members and a new Executive was appointed.[63] The study program was also changed so that the work was given to Task Forces which were grouped into a simplified system of four Study Units. Two key Study Units came under new leadership – Chris Sugden was suddenly replaced in his work with the Ethics and Society Unit by Dr Bong Ho Son of Korea, while Rolf Hille of Germany took over leadership of the Faith and Church Unit. Other units were Theology of Missions and Evangelism (Bishop Gbonigi) and Church and Ministry (Rev. Rene Daidanso). The next consultation was set down for Guatemala in 1995, but many other events intervened to prevent that idea ever coming to fruition.

Ethics and environment

A second major consultation for the year took place 26-31 August, 1992. It was conducted by the Ethics and Society Unit, and led by the outgoing convenor, Chris Sugden, in conjunction with the Au Sable Institute of Environmental Studies at its centre near Mancelona, Michigan, USA. The conference was attended by sixty people from eight countries, with the theme, 'Christians caring for creation'. Initiated at the 1990 TC meetings, it was planned as a global response to issues that had been largely neglected by evangelicals and as an opportunity to present an alternate and more biblically balanced view than those which had emerged in other settings.[64] This consultation was the last productive effort of the Ethics and Society Unit, concluding a long series of stimulating projects.

---

[63] The Executive was Dr P. Kuzmič (chair), R. Daidanso (vice-chair), R. Hille, W. Gasque, E. Gbonigi, P. Arana, Bong Ho Son (replacing W. Chow), with Bong Rin Ro as Executive Director, R. Kemp (ICAA) and B. J. Nicholls (Editor, *ERT*).

[64] A lengthy statement 'Evangelical Christianity and the environment' was prepared and published in an expanded version of *ERT* 17:2 (April 1993), along with eleven papers; the statement was also published as No. 7 of the TC 'Outreach and Identity' monograph series in 1993; see also *Transformation* Vol 9 No 4 (Oct-Dec 1992), pp. 27-30.

Chapter V Serving the Church

Change of focus

The previous two or three years had been filled with a busy round of activities and initiatives which were effectively restoring the thrust of the Commission as a global organization committed to advancing evangelical theology as a basis for discerning the obedience of faith. However, late in 1992, there was an announcement of an important development which was intended to result in a significant new focus for its work. The concept had much to commend it, but in the context of the changes and challenges already facing the organization, it would have a disturbing effect.

At a meeting of WEF staff in December 1992, Dr Augustin ('Jun') Vencer[65] who had become the WEF International Director at the General Assembly earlier in the year, presented his vision for the entire organization in terms of 'new target.' By this he meant that the work of the WEF would become strongly directed towards strengthening National Evangelical Fellowships (NEFs), of which there were now about seventy.[66] His strategy involved global networking, defining programs and replicating WEF ministries at the national level, and especially leadership development at national and local levels. The Commissions were an integral part of this plan.

This meant that the emphasis of the TC would now be not so much on working with theologians, seminaries and theological associations. Instead, as TN reported,[67] it would 'work closely with national evangelical fellowships which in turn would strengthen the respective national theological commissions,' although as the report conceded, the TC 'must not also overlook the existing regional theological associations with which it had been associated in past years ... ' It would also need to change from working on traditional theological topics to focus on training national

---

[65] Jun Vencer with John Allan, *Poor is no Excuse: the story of Jun Vencer* (Exeter/Grand Rapids: Paternoster/; Grand Rapids : Baker Book House, 1989. Vencer, a lawyer and ordained pastor, was previously Executive Director of the Philippines Council of Evangelical Churches, and served on the WEF International Council as well as many other national and international organisations.

[66] See also Jun Vencer, 'Churches transforming the nations: the DNA vision', ERT 24:4 (Dec 2000), pp. 301-327; 'New Direction for Theological Commission', TN Vol 25 No 1 (Jan—Mar 1995), p. 5.

[67] TN Vol 24 No 1 (Jan-Mar 1993), p. 1f.

church leadership, and on the development of faculty, library and plant in seminaries.

These plans, which reflected views on theological education published by Vencer much earlier,[68] were adopted strongly by Bong Ro. In his efforts to 'change the status quo' of the TC, he was supported by the WEF North American Director, Galen Hiestand, with whom he had conferred at length.[69] The pair of them had extensive discussions with Overseas Council about the future of the scholarship scheme. These new ideas were presented to the TC Executive during 1993 in the form of recommendations about an 'Evangelical Leadership Development Fund'.

One important consequence of this plan for the TC to be much more directly involved in theological education would be overlap with the ICAA and its constituency. However, the TC did not have the ability to generate the resources needed to fund such ambitious plans as these, which was left to other more specialised groups such as the Overseas Council and the Langham Trust.

At the time, the ICAA itself was moving more towards its goal of being a 'full service agency' for evangelical theological education, rather than merely an association of accrediting agencies. This process was advanced by its 1993 Consultation held 19-23 July in Bangkok, Thailand on the theme, 'Affirming the Spectrum: Doing Theological Education Together.' This development meant that there was less reason for the TC to work directly in theological education. This trend, together with the decline of key study units like Faith and Church and Ethics and Society, meant that TC would need a new vision to avoid losing its way altogether.

The TC's relationships with theological associations and other institutions in various parts of the world were also becoming more tenuous, especially in the light of the continuing reluctance by some of the current WEF leadership to support the values they fostered. The inevitable result was that these regional associations found other more supportive alliances, and so turned their attention away from the TC and the WEF itself. In any case, the regional theological associations had their own distinctive history and ethos, and there was no official organizational relationship with TC which could be used to foster support for its work.

---

[68] TN/TET Vol 19 No 4 (Oct-Dec 1987).
[69] *Evangelical World*, July 1993, p. 7. 'Up to now, the TC has been issue oriented.... .But after these two years of thinking and reflection, Dr Ro is to change the status quo. ... Dr Ro would like to see the WEF Theological Commission, working closely with regional and national evangelical associations, identify and adopt theological institutions in each country and develop them to a level where they can offer good theological education.'

In these circumstances, the only hope of formal support for the TC was by relating to the national evangelical fellowships. However, as reports of the previous decade acknowledged, many of them were not strong, and few had any kind of theological work as part of their program. Thus the networking and supportive role envisaged by the Vencer plan would have to be a long term one.

A TC Executive meeting at which this change in focus could have been discussed was planned to take place in association with this ICAA consultation in Thailand in July 1993, but it was cancelled due to the inability of several members to attend. This denied the TC the decisive leadership it needed to cope with the challenges of the proposed new direction. It also meant that the TC leadership was not able to respond adequately to the unmistakeable slow down in Study Unit activity at that time. However, the TC Scholarships committee did meet to consider applications, but shortage of funds meant that little progress took place.

Publications and consultations

Despite this, 1993 was a year of advance in the publications. Bong Ro was responsible for a significant expansion of the monograph (or Occasional Papers) 'Outreach and Identity' series which had not seen any activity for a decade. He added five titles in this period.[70] Although there was some misunderstanding about the status of the series and the propriety of this move, the rush of publications was welcome, especially since some important statements of TC consultations were made available to interested readers. But no more followed, and the series itself was not developed any further after this.

The volume on the WCC Assembly, *Beyond Canberra,* was also published by Regnum Books[71] in association with Lynx Communications (SPCK) in March 1993, and the papers from the 1992 TC Consultation were being edited. Executive member, Pedro Arana (Peru), also translated some of the monographs into Spanish for wider distribution in Latin America.

---

[70] They were: *The Unique Christ in our Pluralistic World* (The 1992 WEF Manila Declaration); *An Evangelical response to 'Confessing the one Faith'* (WEF TC Ecumenical Issues Task Force, 1992); *Evangelical Christianity and the Environment* (WEF TC Ethics and Society Study Unit and Au Sable Institute consultation, 1992); *Toward a Theology of Theological Education* by Dieumeme Noelliste (ICAA Consultation, 1993); *Sharing the Good News with the Poor* (1993 WEF Consultation Statement).

[71] Regnum Books are third-world publishers associated with the Oxford Centre for Mission Studies.

Bong Ro was busy preparing a large number of entries for a *World Directory of Theological Institutions* which he proposed to publish. This was an ambitious attempt to catalogue the entire global scene, an enlarged version of similar directories that he had produced earlier for the Asian region. However, it became a matter of concern to the TC Executive because its inclusive nature seemed to endorse indiscriminately all seminaries listed regardless of their theological positions. Therefore, in the end, it was not endorsed as an official TC publication. The first edition, covering 4000 institutions, was published privately in June 1994, and second expanded edition appeared in the following year.

One other successful venture in 1993 was the consultation on the 'Evangelization of the Poor', originally sponsored by the Ethics and Society Unit. It was planned to follow up an idea made by the AD2000 movement and to build on earlier efforts of evangelicals to 'discern the theology of evangelization that is expressed in the practice of Christian ministries among the poor, and the practice that best expresses a biblical theology of evangelization among the poor.' The new Study Unit convenor, Dr Bong Ho Son, was not able to organize it, so Dr Bruce Nicholls took over this task. It was held 17-23 October in New Delhi with twenty-five people, including theologians, relief workers and pastors gathering from ten countries, who presented papers and also made field trips to development projects and slum areas to gain a first hand understanding of the topic.

Participants were struck by the abject poverty of slum dwellers in many parts of Asia and the world, and the corresponding lack of interest shown in their spiritual needs. So they saw an urgent need to re-evaluate the theological basis for Christian social ministries, and to establish an emphasis on evangelism and church planting as well as the provision of food and shelter, This would mean local churches should be involved in Christian social responsibilities in their areas, and that pastors and church leaders should be better trained in understanding poverty and suffering.[72]

Another continuing sign of significant activity was seen in the Ecumenical Issues Task Force. Following the preliminary talks between the WEF leadership and the Roman Catholic Church in 1988 and 1990, the next phase in the conversations between the two bodies took place at Venice 21-25 October, 1993, consisting of a carefully prepared consultation. The topics discussed were Scripture and Tradition, and Justification

---

[72] Papers were published in ERT 18:2 (Apr 1994), and in B. J. Nicholls and Beulah R. Woods (editors), *Sharing Good News with the Poor* (Carlisle: Paternoster, 1996).

by Faith. No official statement was made, but the papers and responses were subsequently published in ERT.[73] These talks indicated that there were two other pressing topics that divided the groups which merited discussion – the nature of the church as communion, and the nature and practice of mission and evangelism. These would be the subject of later meetings.

The early 1990s had been a busy and productive time for the TC under the energetic leadership of Bong Ro, but as the organization approached its twentieth anniversary in 1994, there would be a striking change.

TC at twenty years

Despite a busy and productive year in 1993, the Executive of the Theological Commission had not met to guide its activities. This meant that it did not have the opportunity to address the significant changes to its role that had been proposed by the WEF changing it from a body committed primarily to theological reflection to one working at the grassroots level in leadership development and training. This disturbance was symptomatic of more to come during the twentieth year of the organization's history.

The TC Executive finally met at Elburn, Illinois 7-10 January, 1994 with a large agenda, catching up the backlog since the previous meeting a year and a half earlier in Manila. In particular, WEF International Director Jun Vencer personally presented his new vision for the TC, and urged the TC to fall into line with moves towards greater integration and unity which were taking place within the WEF. Dr Bong Rin Ro (now known as Executive Director) reinforced this policy by proposing a threefold plan – tackling major theological issues through the Study Unit program, training church leaders and strengthening national evangelical fellowships.

He emphasised that the TC could accomplish its accreditation work and the establishment of seminaries through the ICAA, but there was a need to expand the scholarship and library development schemes, and to work through national alliances and developing networks of theologians, including the encouragement of younger ones. He urged the establishment of the previously proposed Evangelical Leadership Development Fund to meet the great demand for financial resources, and to work closely with groups such as Overseas Council and the Langham Trust who were also involved in supporting theological education globally. Howev-

---

[73] ERT 21:2 (April 1997), pp. 101-154) under the theme, *Justification, Scripture and Tradition*.

er, the Executive concluded that his suggestion about the TC conducting seminars in churches was one that needed more thought because it was doubtful that it was appropriate for the TC as a global body to be working at this local level.

Publications were again a major concern at this Executive meeting, with serious consideration being given to the plans of the WEF Publications Commission for a coordinated approach to the task, and also to the idea of expanding TC publications into various world languages. Although *Beyond Canberra* had finally appeared, there was uncertainty about whether the book from the 1992 consultation could be funded by Paternoster Press. However approval was given to publish the papers from the consultation on the Evangelisation of the Poor when the issue of the Canberra book had been clarified. Bruce Nicholls would now be assisted in his work as editor of *Evangelical Review of Theology* by two new appointments – Dr John Roxborogh, a missiologist from the Bible College of New Zealand, as Associate Editor, and TC member and theologian, Dr David Parker (Australia) as Book Review Editor. *Theological News* continued to be supported financially but there were no issues published in 1994.

There was little to report from the Study Units (apart from Ecumenical Issues) – they seemed to have run out of momentum. Finances were very difficult. No new Scholarship applications were considered.

Nevertheless, some concrete plans were laid for the future with a decision to endorse and co-sponsor with the Overseas Council the Consultation of Theological Education Leaders of Schools in the Post-Communist world at Oradea, Romania, 4-7 October, 1994. This proved to be a highly constructive event in helping to develop a vision for theological education in the region. In addition, there was a commitment by the participants to the creation of an organizational structure to facilitate study, faculty development, networking, research and publication. As a result of these efforts, the East European Accrediting Association was formed in 1997 with more than forty members and duly became a constituent of ICAA (or ICETE as it was known by then).

The next TC consultation and general meeting was due in 1995, but these events were deferred because of the major plans for the WEF General Assembly the following year. In any case, the large impact that GCOWE II would have on the global evangelical constituency made such a decision a necessity.[74]

---

[74] GCOWE II was held 17-25 May, 1995 at the Korean Center for World Mission, attracting nearly 4,000 Christian leaders representing 186 nations, and was regarded as a highly significant event, especially for third-world Christians.

Pace slackens

There was a positive mood and plenty of ideas for the development of the TC at the January meeting in Elburn, but these hopeful signs did not translate into action. Instead the rest of 1994 was characterised by a marked slowdown in TC operations. Bong Ro was often on the move travelling, and he had also expanded his teaching responsibilities at ACTS. In addition, he was now Overseas Ministry Director for the Korean Center for World Missions; he hoped this activity might develop local support for the TC, especially in the area of publications, but nothing concrete emerged. Plans to hold a second meeting of the TC Executive in 1994, this time in Seoul in association with a consultation on 'Prosperity Theology and the Theology of Suffering', were also part of this strategy.

This consultation was speedily arranged with the enthusiastic interest and support of the Korea Evangelical Theological Society. Despite the short time for preparation, it was highly successful, attracting fifty people including the TC Executive members who participated fully. There were seven major papers from biblical, theological and geographical perspectives. There was also a lengthy statement pointing out, among other matters, the suitability of holding such a consultation in Korea which, 'having passed through the fires of intense persecution and suffering during the first part of this century, has become quite prosperous and is rapidly becoming one of the dominant sending churches in the world Christian mission.'[75]

The Executive meeting, held 26-28 September just before the Consultation, was well attended, but reports confirmed that TC activity was weak and many of the initiatives from the previous meeting had not been pursued. The outlook for scholarships continued to be poor, and no new offers were made. In fact, applicants had been referred to the Overseas Council.

There was little substantial Study Unit activity to report, with the exception of the Ecumenical Issues Unit. It had met 23-26 May, 1994 for the Scripture and Tradition project, first established in 1992, and now had material ready for publication.[76] The Convenor, Dr Paul Schrotenboer, also advised that he had been informed that the conversations with the Roman Catholic Church would be moved from the responsibility of the WEF International Director (where they had lain since the beginning), and would now come under the direct control of the TC. He hoped this

---

[75] The papers were published in *ERT* 20:1 (Jan 1996).
[76] *ERT* 19:2 (April 1995).

arrangement would make for smoother and more efficient administration.

Publications was one area in which there was a more positive outlook. After the multiple additions to the monograph series in 1993, the full length book of the 1992 consultation, *The Unique Christ in our Pluralistic World* would appear in October 1994, and work on the book from the consultation on the Evangelization of the Poor (1993) was well advanced.

The biggest matter facing the TC Executive was the next general meeting and consultation, which were scheduled for 1996 when the 10th WEF General Assembly was scheduled. Due to restrictions on the amount of time Dr Ro was able to give to TC matters, Dr Bruce Nicholls was appointed to organize the consultation, and his initial proposals about speakers and funding were endorsed. Dr David Parker of Australia was also appointed as an assistant to Dr Nicholls for the consultation organization in addition to his work with *ERT*.

The Chairman, Dr Peter Kuzmič, was also struggling to find time to devote to TC work because he was increasingly involved in the worsening military and political conditions in his homeland area. He was also much in demand as an international speaker, and now had responsibilities as a professor at Gordon Conwell Theological Seminary, Boston, USA, where he had taken up a prestigious appointment in 1993.

Over the next few months, interest was focused mainly on preparations for the 1996 consultation, most other activities having seriously declined. Dr Paul Schrotenboer was looking for a decision from the TC Executive on the next stage of the talks with the Roman Catholic Church. The Ethics and Society Unit was planning for a further consultation to be held in Korea early in 1996 on the vexed topic of bribery, but because of organizational problems, it failed to eventuate. *TN* appeared again in early 1995 after a year's break and there was some hope of better publishing arrangements after top level talks in March and April 1995 between WEF and Paternoster (which in July 1992 had become the theological publishing arm of the STL group within Operation Mobilization[77]). The ICAA developed an increasing sense of purpose, which was reflected in news that it was considering adopting a new name that would be more descriptive of its functions as an autonomous full service organization.

---

[77] For more on STL, see page 113.

New focus at Prague

These developments meant that decisive action was required by the TC Executive when it met next in Prague, 3-5 April, 1995. It was a small session, with only five members present, apologies being received from Ward Gasque, Bong Ho Son and Bishop Gbonigi. Roger Kemp represented the ICAA. Dr Jun Vencer, WEF International Director, was present to reinforce his views about the new vision and strategies for the TC, and to give details about how the commissions were expected to integrate with the forthcoming General Assembly. It was clear that the most important task of the meeting was to focus on organizing a stimulating consultation and to plan for a TC meeting that would provide a launching pad for the revival of the Commission.

With just one year to go, the Executive endorsed the plans which had been developed by Dr Bruce Nicholls and Dr David Parker for a consultation which would have as its theme, 'Faith and Hope for the Future: Towards a vital and coherent theology for the 21st Century.' There was a strong emphasis on gaining the active involvement of TC members with whom there had been little contact for some time; it was also planned to broaden the scope of the TC by attracting representatives from national fellowships and other key theological bodies. It was hoped that these strategies would provide new personnel, effective leadership and a program of activities which would allow the TC to resume its positive thrust once again after several years of reduced activity.

Decisions were also necessary on the leadership of the TC. Dr Peter Kuzmič's term as Chairman would expire in 1996. Furthermore, as Dr Bong Ro was due to take a year's furlough from mid-1995, it was decided that he would conclude his active involvement as TC Executive Director at that point. Dr David Parker was appointed Honorary Administrator to prepare for the 1996 Consultation and general meeting. Dr Bong Ro would be officially farewelled at the consultation.

The future vitality of the TC now depended on a successful consultation in April 1996 and the appointment of a new Executive Director who could develop its potential. However, there was a great deal to be done to prepare the TC for this new opportunity. With Ro's departure on furlough, the TC office in Seoul was closed on 31 July, 1995, and a thorough review of the TC organization, finances and programs began. Regular publication of *TN* was continued in the form of a modest four-page xeroxed edition issued quarterly.

There was a good response to preparation for the consultation which was originally planned to take place in conjunction with WEF General Assembly (and other Commission meetings) at Minehead, Somerset, UK. This event, in turn, was to be part of the large Spring Harvest convention which took place there every year.

However, a major interruption to preparations occurred in late June 1995 when the WEF administration advised its constituency that it had encountered serious financial problems because of the collapse of a pyramid type fund raising scheme in USA.[78] Furthermore, the GCOWE conference in Seoul, Korea in May 1995 created divided loyalties amongst the constituency for a major world conference. There were also concerns about the cost and other arrangements at the venue in Minehead. The WEF leadership therefore announced that it was postponing the Assembly to a date and place to be decided. This had a major impact on the Commissions which were already well advanced in their planning.

The TC decided to go ahead with its Consultation at the same time as originally planned, but at another site. Soon, arrangements were providentially made to hold it at London Bible College[79] (LBC), Northwood, London, 9-15 April, 1996. By moving to London Bible College, the Theological Commission was returning to its roots at a crucial time in its history. The first consultation and full meeting ever conducted by the Commission was held at LBC in 1975.

The new location and circumstances proved to be advantageous, and as preprations drew to a close early in 1996 and the review of TC administration was completed, there was mounting expectation of an outcome that would match the theme selected for the occasion, 'Faith and Hope for the Future.'

'Faith and Hope for the Future'

The Consultation was attended by about one hundred people from virtually every major area of the world. Many had long associations with the TC, but others were first timers, and a good number represented national Evangelical Fellowships. The aim of the conference was to prepare papers and a final consultation statement analysing contemporary trends in the light of the theme, 'Towards a Vital and Coherent Evangelical Theology for the 21st Century,' identifying key issues for evangelical theology and proposing responses on a global basis across a range of topics.

---

[78] The collapse of the Foundation for New Era Philanthropy in May 1995 was reported in *Christianity Today* 19 June and 17 July, 1995.

[79] LBC is now known as London School of Theology

Chapter V Serving the Church

Participants were divided into twelve working groups, one for each of the sub-topics of the theme; they covered the entire range of theology and touched on relevant contemporary issues in fields such as mission, ethics, contextualisation, ecology, discipleship and gender distinctions. It was intended that the findings would provide useful insights for the evangelical public and guidelines for future theological reflection. In particular, they would provide the essence of a program for the TC Study Units in the following triennium.

The consultation was an outstanding success, and the reports of the working groups produced statements which provided promising materials for future development. The group reports and plenary papers were published in ERT.[80] Participants were encouraged to volunteer to take the process further by forming on-going groups that would continue to meet after the consultation with the intention of producing full sized reports. As it turned out, only one of the groups was able to reach the stage of publication.

With so little activity in the recent past, the main function of the general TC meeting held at the Consultation was to plan for the future. The arrival of the outgoing chairman, Peter Kuzmič was delayed because of his involvement in activities related to the political situation in his homeland. It was hoped that the long run down in support for the Scholarship program, which was now virtually defunct, would be reversed by asking the ICAA to take responsibility for it, especially since the program was originally designed as a way of developing the faculty of theological institutions. However, a message from the ICAA which was meeting simultaneously at Moorlands Bible College, Sopley, Dorset, about one hundred miles away, indicated that the scheme was not high on its priorities and it was unable to take responsibility for it. So the program was suspended indefinitely, after a life of seventeen years during which many students and their schools had been assisted. Shortage of funds in later years in particular had limited its effectiveness.

A slate of new TC members was proposed, numbering about fifty with a good global coverage, in the pattern that had been established over the years. A new Executive was appointed,[81] with Dr Rolf Hille of Germany as

---

[80] ERT 20:4 (Oct 1996) and Vol 21 No 1 (Jan 1997) contained the papers and working group statements.
[81] P. Kuzmič, E. Gbonigi, Bong Ho Son concluded their terms of service; R Hille (Germany), P. Arana (Peru), R Daidanso (Chad), and W. Gasque (Canada) continued, and were joined by Judith Gundry-Volf (USA), K. Gnanakan (India) and Bong R. Ro (the former Executive Director, Korea).

the chairman. Dr Hille had joined the Executive first in 1986 and had served on several study units. He had been on the faculty of Albrecht Bengel Haus, Tuebingen since 1995, and would soon be made rector of this strategic institution. He was Chairman of the German Evangelical Alliance, and was active in other national and regional theological and evangelical bodies. He was a respected member of the Evangelical Lutheran Church in Wuerttemberg (ELCW), which had long supported the work of WEF, and the TC in particular.

Dr Bong Rin Ro concluded his term of service as Executive Director at this conference and was honoured for his seven years of work. In the first stage, he had skilfully balanced several responsibilities and succeeded in giving a great deal of hope for the TC, despite being engaged only on an interim part-time basis. After being appointed on a full-time basis and returning to Korea, his passion, energy and vision produced a flood of activity, but from about 1992, new concepts and a variety of extraneous influences resulted in a loss of focus. Bong Ro himself gave increasing time to important local activities such a seminary teaching and missions leadership. These were pursuits that he would be free to pursue more fully in the time following his furlough leading up to his retirement in 1999, and beyond.

Dr David Parker's role as Administrator also concluded. However, the Search Committee had not been able to bring forward a nomination for a new Executive Director, so until a new appointment could be made, Dr Hille became Executive Chairman responsible for both the overall leadership and the day to day administration of the TC. He soon appointed James Kautt of Tuebingen as his administrative assistant making it possible for him to carry out this demanding dual role as well as maintaining his other responsibilities, especially as head of Bengel Haus.

Other members of the Executive members were also expected to share some of the work load. Dr Bruce Nicholls remained as editor of *ERT*, and Dr Hille took temporary responsibility for *TN*. A priority for the Executive was the search for a new Director, who it was hoped could be appointed at the next meeting due to be held in conjunction with the rescheduled WEF General Assembly a year later in Canada. A mini-consultation would also be held at that time.

Immediately following the Consultation, two other meetings took place which were intended to boost the work of the TC and its cooperation with the wider WEF family – a gathering evangelical publishers with the aim of increasing cooperation, especially between western and third world organizations, and an informal joint meeting of Commission leaders. It was hoped that this latter meeting especially would capture some of the intentions behind the original plan of holding the Commission meetings together at Minehead during the General Assembly period.

During this session, representatives from the accrediting associations announced that ICAA had changed its name to The International Council for Evangelical Theological Education (ICETE), which was a better indication of the new function towards which it had been working for several years. It was now officially an organization, operating under the auspices of the WEF (not the TC), serving the entire needs of theological education, rather than accreditation alone – as its mission statement put it, 'Strengthening evangelical theological education through international contact and cooperation.' This meant that ICETE would be free to pursue its own activities while maintaining loose links to WEF. Financially it was hoped that earlier experience would repeat itself when it received greater support as an independent body than when funding was channelled through WEF and TC.

During the TC consultation and other meetings, there had been many good ideas for the development of the TC, and it seemed as if there had been a genuine recovery of 'faith and hope for the future.' But it would be a struggle, with many setbacks and disappointments yet before the way forward seemed clear again. ICETE too had found a new vision, but its finances were poor and the General Secretary, Dr Roger Kemp, announced he would soon conclude his service. After he did so in May 1997, completing an eight year term, ICETE was not represented at TC Executive meetings as it had been from its inception. Hence the two organizations began to drift apart, which would once again raise the need for talks to reestablish a closer working relationship.

Chapter VI Networking Theologians

Revisioning at Pasadena 1996

There was little TC activity during the rest of 1996 – only one issue of *TN* was published, but new Executive member, Dr Judy Gundry-Volf, arranged for the Executive to meet in December at Fuller Theological Seminary, Pasadena, California, where she taught New Testament. Ward Gasque, Ken Gnanakan, Judith Gundry-Volf, Bong Ro and Rolf Hille attended, the WEF leadership was represented for some of the time by Dwight Gibson, North American Director, and Roger Kemp was present for ICETE. This strategic venue provided opportunity for interaction with some important theologians, including Dr Richard Mouw, President of the seminary and Dr William Dyrness; former TC Executive Secretary, Dr Sunand Sumithra, who was visiting the seminary, shared details of his current research project.

During the business sessions there began to develop a new vision of the TC as a body networking with other theological associations and institutions, national evangelical fellowships and churches, as well as a group of individuals. The Study Units would be re-focused with this new approach in mind. The membership was reviewed and the scholarship program was formally terminated with the hope that the gap might be filled by other organizations, a wish that was more than adequately realised in the rapid growth of the Langham Scholarship scheme.

Although there was little information available from the WEF office about the financial situation, the Executive pressed ahead with a new budget and creative plans for publications, involvement in the 1997 General Assembly program, joint meetings with the Interchurch Relief and Development Alliance (IRDA), and a 'World Forum on Evangelical Theology.' The situation in Hong Kong after its re-unification with China in 1997 was also a topic of concern. However, there was no definite progress on the most important question of all – the appointment of a new Executive Director. Some general ideas were discussed and various names were suggested, but the adoption of a job description would have to wait.

Nevertheless, the ideas for a new vision ventilated at Pasadena were taken a step forward by chairman Dr Rolf Hille and vice-chairman Dr Ken Gnanakan, when they met at Tuebingen in two months later, February, 1997. After a period of intense discussion, they drew up a seven-page position paper titled, 'A comprehensive vision for the Theological Commission of the WEF.' The vision centred on the TC being transformed from an established commission of about fifty members into a dynamic international network of theologians and institutions. The emphasis would change from large periodic consultations to flexible ongoing activities, aided by the growing availability of electronic mail and the internet. This paper became the major source of ideas for the next Executive meeting planned to be held just prior to the postponed WEF General Assembly, which was now set down for Abbotsford, near Vancouver, Canada in 6-9 May, 1997. The general ideas in this document guided the development of the TC into the years ahead.

Abbotsford 1997

However, arrangements for the TC meeting at the Abbotsford Assembly were thrown into turmoil when the chairman, Dr Hille was struck with a family tragedy immediately prior to the meeting and was unable to attend. In his absence, informal talks were held, attended by the other Executive members and several visitors. During the 'think-tank' that this meeting became, the general ideas expressed at the Pasadena meeting and reflected in the 'Comprehensive Vision' paper were studied and supported in principle. It was realised that the TC should focus on its main calling of theological reflection, which meant that subsidiary activities such as theological education and scholarship funding could be left to other bodies, especially ICETE. This represent a considerable change of direction from the policies being considered earlier in the 1990s, in which the focus was more on the training of local church leaders.

Ken Gnanakan was given charge of the study unit program which needed to be refocused to fit in with the new approach. Only one of the groups from the 1996 Consultation was still active, and none of the previous Units was operative. So it was decided to set up a small coordinating group to develop this area of the work.

Arrangements for the TC publications, especially *ERT*, were a matter of considerable concern. It was hoped that with the expansion of the TC's role and changes in is mode of operation, *ERT* would take on added significance, perhaps even with non-English versions, and that an enlargement of its circulation could lead to better subscription pricing. Dr Bruce Nicholls called for urgent action to develop the publications work, but at the same time indicated that he was available as editor only for a further year

Financial considerations were critical to the implementation of the new vision, but prospects were not good. It was decided to approach the

North American WEF Director for assistance, and consideration was given to introducing membership fees for individuals and institutions. There was still no possibility for the immediate appointment of an Executive Director, so the existing administrative arrangements were maintained.

In an effort to revive the study unit activity which had been so important earlier, Dr Ken Gnanakan met with Dr Paul Murdoch (Germany) and Dr Brian Edgar (Australia) at Wheaton in January 1998. They prepared a wide-ranging report which advocated a dynamic program of interaction between up to 500 theologians using electronic communication in a community atmosphere. They would produce papers and statements relating to immediate concerns facing the evangelical world, on-going issues relative to local communities and reflecting on evangelical identity. These documents would be circulated in the most efficient means possible and be directed towards the WEF and its membership and constituency, as well as other publications and groups. The team identified five areas on which work could commence immediately under the leadership of TC-related personnel, including the team members themselves. If these plans eventuated, the TC would be well on the way to re-establishing itself with a new updated modus operandi.

The long awaited next phase of the WEF/Roman Catholic Church talks were held 12-19 October, 1997 at Tantur Ecumenical Institute in Jerusalem on the theme, 'The nature and mission of the church.' Increasing mutual confidence between the two partners was reflected in the fact that for the first time a communiqué about this meeting was published.[82]

Tuebingen 1998

By the time of the next Executive Committee meeting, held at Tuebingen, Germany 28 May to 2 June, 1998,[83] there was considerable expectation that the worst was behind the TC. Publication of *TN* had resumed under the leadership of Dr Ken Gnanakan with regular four-page issues appearing quarterly throughout 1997. Dr David Parker was appointed editor of *ERT* to replace Dr Bruce Nicholls who would retire at the end of the year.

---

[82] The communiqué and papers were published both in the *ERT* 23:1 (Jan 1999) and *One in Christ*, 35:1 (1999), pp. 11-92.

[83] Present were Executive members R. Hille, K. Gnanakan, Bong Ro, Ward Gasque and Pedro Arana. There were also seven invited guests including B. J. Nicholls and D. Parker, and others who were potential TC members or contributors to its study program. D. Gibson, North American WEF Director represented the WEF International Director.

However, by this time, the need for a full time Executive Director was becoming urgent. Notices placed in *TN* and elsewhere resulted in several enquiries. Preliminary steps were being taken for another general consultation to be held in 1999.

The major business for the Executive was the adoption of the new concept for the structure and work of the TC, and some of the ideas in the report of the Wheaton task force. This meant the TC would be seen as a large representative community of theologians endorsed by their national fellowships which would work primarily through study groups and dynamic task forces. There would be a core group of about twenty-five representing a regional cross-section and able to network effectively in their own areas who would take responsibility and give time to specific aspects of the work. An executive of five plus the Executive Director and WEF International Director would supervise policy and business.

The Ecumenical Issues Task Force was the object of special attention due to news of a serious decline in the health of its long-time convenor, Dr Paul Schrotenboer. It was agreed that the momentum of previous activities should not be lost. Accordingly, Dr George Vandervelde (Canada), who had been involved over a lengthy period, was appointed as the new convenor with approval to continue the talks later in the year. Only a few weeks later Dr Paul Schrotenboer[84] died. His deep commitment to the process was reflected in the fact that throughout the whole series of meetings he was struggling with his health and in the latter stages, physical disability.

However, despite these positive and forward-looking plans, the financial situation was still dismal. The appointment of a Director was critical to the success of efforts towards renewal, but there was no chance of paying a salary; it was hoped that this would not be necessary as all the previous appointees had been supported by outside sources.

---

[84] Dr. Paul G. Schrotenboer, a minister of the Christian Reformed Church, was part-time development director of the Association for the Advancement of Christian Scholarship (now Institute for Christian Studies, Toronto, Canada), and in 1966 became General Secretary of the Reformed Ecumenical Synod (later Council). In this post for 25 years, he carried out distinguished work in North America and on the world scene, especially in relationship with the issue of apartheid in South Africa.

New director

Efforts prior to and also during the 1998 Executive meeting to find a suitable appointee were unsuccessful. But some progress was made when it was realised that Dr James Stamoolis, who was about to conclude as Dean of Wheaton Graduate School, might be available. He was well known to some of the members already, and in addition, was a TC member and had been leading the Orthodox Task Force. Previously he had been Theological Student Fellowship Secretary for the International Fellowship of Evangelical Students (IFES), which gave him responsibility for assisting the national Christian student associations in more than a hundred countries. For several years prior to his IFES work, he had worked in mission appointments in theological education in South Africa. During this time he gained his doctorate from the University of Stellenbosch specialising in Eastern Orthodox missiology.

This background made him an attractive candidate, so negotiations were opened up with him, on the assurances of the North American office and himself that funds could be raised from new sources for his support and for the general TC budget. The TC Chairman welcomed the possibility of appointing Dr Stamoolis, but realistically offered only limited financial support from TC sources as a bridge until the new funding was found. According to WEF procedures, Jun Vencer as International Director then proceeded to make the appointment. The new Director took up his position in October 1998, thus ending a gap of more than three years since the last director had concluded his activities. Living in Wheaton, Stamoolis was able to relate closely to the North American WEF office, headed by Dwight Gibson, located at nearby Carol Stream.

Now it was expected that plans for the new core group, study units, networks and consultations that had been developed at meetings going back to Pasadena December 1996 would begin to materialise. Dr Hille could step back from the dual role of Chairman and Administrator. Using a system described by Dr Ken Gnanakan as 'Cyberlogue', it was hoped to make increased use of internet facilities for networking of theologians by expanding the TC web-site set up two years earlier by David Parker. Parker also took over as *ERT* editor from the January 1998 issue, with an increasing focus on the journal as a forum of the now flourishing global evangelical theological scholarship. However, it was more difficult to tackle the continuing problems of high subscription costs and lower than desired circulation – problems that Dr Stamoolis began to address.

The next opportunity to develop and focus the work was at the Executive meeting held in Jamaica in February 1999; it was held at this location to take advantage of the opportunity to network with members of the WEA leadership and also of the Caribbean Evangelical Association who would all be meeting there at the time. Although the meeting was poorly attended, the new Director was able to review in detail the work of the TC with the officers who were present. WEF officials who were attending other meetings at the same venue helped with an analysis of finances and related matters. Dr David Parker who was attending in his capacity as editor of *ERT* was confirmed in this position since Dr Stamoolis indicated he was not intending to take over this aspect of the work; Dr Parker was also appointed to the Executive. Dr Stamoolis took charge of the Study Units, in association with Dr Hille and Dr Gnanakan. One satisfying feature was the report that the eschatology work group from the 1996 London consultation, led by Dr Jochen Eber (Switzerland), was close to publishing its book. There was also productive discussion about the talks proceeding with the Roman Catholic Church and preliminary ideas were aired about similar meetings with the Orthodox.

Wide ranging projects

The Jamaica meeting laid the groundwork for the continued development of the TC under an Executive Director who could give the program focus, purpose and continuity along the lines previously developed. During the subsequent months, Dr Stamoolis became involved in a number of other activities on behalf of the WEF. One of these was the Global Consultation on Evangelical Missiology organized by WEF Missions Commission at Iguassu, Brazil in October 1999. Another was an international leadership conference organized by WEF and held in Larnaca, Cyprus in 21-24 February, 2000, in which, at the direction of the WEF leadership, he took a key role in planning and leadership.

Perhaps the most far reaching of these other activities was the Conference of Itinerant Evangelists sponsored by Billy Graham, to be held in Amsterdam in August 2000, involving 10,000 participants. Dr Stamoolis believed that the theology track of this conference provided a strategic opportunity to advance the work of the TC in the area where it needed to be seen, the grassroots level of the church worldwide. Hence he was keen to see members of the TC involved as much as possible, and made strong representations along these lines to Dr Jim Packer who was responsible for this track.

In addition to this, Dr Stamoolis became involved in the preparation of a CD-ROM for distribution to participants to promote the ministry of WEF and as a useful ministry tool. There had been general discussion in the TC about the possibility of putting TC publications on CD-ROM for easy and cost-effective circulation. Due to the destruction of most of the early stock of *ERT* and other publications in the Paternoster fire in 1990, it was an attractive proposition to consider having this material available again in such a handy form. The WEF leadership also saw benefits in the CD-ROM, which eventually contained much more than TC material – a number of books from the WEF itself, some from the Missions Commission, a range of Bibles and other theological books and documents. Finally, 12,000 copies of the CD-ROM were distributed freely to all the participants, where it was a great success. To comply with licensing arrangements, a new, slightly different version was prepared for commercial circulation, and 2,000 copies were produced for release later in the year. Funding of this very costly venture was to come from special appeals and revenue from sales, but a large deficit resulted, even though sales were brisk.

Serious financial and structural difficulties being encountered by the WEF organization itself at the time meant that the TC was obliged to carry this heavy load. This was exacerbated by the need for ongoing financial support for the Executive Director's salary due to the absence of the expected funding from other sources. This left the TC in an even more difficult situation financially. Progress on the other areas of its work like Study Units, Core Group development, networking and consultations was limited, and there was no movement either on improved publication arrangements for *ERT*, despite considerable effort.

Dr Stamoolis' vision for the TC was to make it a 'force to be recognized' globally, and he wanted to bring its operations closer to the life of the churches. This he believed would make it not only more attractive to funding agencies, but also more effective in its role as a WEF commission. But these were long term goals which were not always well understood by others, and so far there was little tangible result from his efforts.

The third session of the WEF/Roman Catholic Church talks was held 7-13 November 1999; at the invitation of WEF they were held at Williams Bay, Wisconsin, USA. By this time it was agreed to proceed with these meetings on a regular basis. This session focused on the theme of the church as communion, and included papers on the important related issues of religious freedom, common witness and proselytism. An important development was the visits by all members of the group to evangelical institutions such as Wheaton College, the Billy Graham Centre and Trinity Evangelical Divinity School on the one hand, and a Roman Catholic seminary in Chicago on the other hand.

Consolidation and vision at Vancouver 2000

The next time the Executive met to review progress of the TC was 29 June – 1 July, 2000 at Regent College, Vancouver, Canada.[85] The Amsterdam conference was soon approaching, so much of Dr Stamoolis's attention was focused on this event, although, as it turned out, there would be little opportunity for direct TC involvement apart from the CD-ROM project. However, the general direction of the TC was consolidated through a review of a paper prepared by Dr Rolf Hille as chairman, 'The Fundamental Strategy of the TC in the future,' which summarised existing thinking. Building on earlier statements, it presented a view of the unique niche into which the TC could fit, bearing in mind the many theological organizations already active at local, national and regional levels, and the limited resources of the TC. It also took account of the role of ICETE as a WEF-related organization devoted to the area of theological education.

This relationship was confirmed in talks between ICETE and the TC chairman, Dr Rolf Hille, in October 2001. This meeting, which was a resumption of formal discussions which had taken place from time to time over many years, issued a statement addressed primarily to the WEA leadership, reaffirming that the two bodies saw themselves as 'distinct entities serving parallel functions within the WEA's objectives and mission' and that they recognized 'distinct but adjacent tasks and the benefit of partnering in specific ways.' It recommitted the TC and ICAA to mutual cooperation and joint activity wherever possible. It also restored the idea of official representation at each other's executive meetings 'for on-going liaison.' It was hoped that this statement would 'adequately address any concerns within WEA that some lingering confusion or tension has been operative between these two WEA bodies.'[86] The Vancouver TC meeting also heard Dr Stamoolis outline his understanding of his role and of his vision for the TC.

The immediate outcome of the review of TC goals and functions by the chairman and the Executive Director was the development of an agreed vision statement which consolidated ideas about the work of the TC itself that had been crystallising over recent meetings. This new

---

[85] R. Hille attended, with K. Gnanakan, W. Gasque, and D. Parker.
[86] Letter of agreement 2 Feb 2002 addressed to the chairman, WEA International Council, jointly signed by ICETE and TC; the document also addressed ICETE's relationship to WEA in that it did not fit easily into either the category of Commission or of Affiliate.

statement[87] summed up the main purpose of the TC in this slogan: '*to promote biblical truth by networking theologians to serve the church in obedience to Christ.*' It explained that the TC would achieve this goal by internationalizing theological frameworks, encouraging original theological reflection and research, defending and confirming the gospel, focusing discussion on practical and relevant themes in varied contexts, and by articulating biblical truth in forms accessible to all Christians.

The means used would be networking evangelical theological organizations and theologians worldwide, organizing theological reflection teams, task forces, study groups, dialogue groups and other international gatherings, and disseminating theological reflection about biblical truth in clear and concise formats for use by the church at all levels.

Throughout the Vancouver meetings, many useful suggestions were made for networking with evangelical bodies and theologians. The understanding was that the Executive Director would follow up with contacts and visits aimed at establishing good relationships and seeking out potential members of the TC and its Study Units. However, despite the adoption of a clear vision of the TC's future ministry, there was still uncertainty about the organizational structures and accountability relationships between the TC, its Executive Director and the WEF leadership. These problems would remain unresolved and continue to cause misunderstandings and difficulties in relationships.

In the meantime, the next year's program was decided. Of particular importance was the 11th WEF General Assembly to be held in Kuala Lumpur. It was hoped that many theologians expected to be present could be attracted to take an interest in the work of the TC. A mini-consultation was planned to precede the Assembly, and there would be joint sessions in the Assembly program with the Commission on Women's Concerns. The Study Unit program was again reviewed, with decisions made about further ecumenical talks, a project on environmental issues, a series of conferences on Church and Education, and the revision of the WEF statement of faith. Publications again received considerable attention. Dr David Parker was appointed to the additional post of editor of *Theological News*, with the task of re-establishing the journal which had not appeared for some time.[88]

The fourth meeting of the WEF/Roman Catholic talks took place at Mundelein, Illinois, 18-24 February, 2001. The evolution of this dialogue

---

[87] See Appendix A.
[88] Publication of *TN* resumed again in January 2001, as a 4-page xeroxed quarterly; only one issue had appeared since Dec 1998.

was reflected in the fact that for the first time it had before it an initial draft of a common text, namely, on the theme of *koinonia* (fellowship), developed by Avery Dulles in cooperation with Henri Blocher (Faculté Libre de Théologie Évangélique, Vaux-sur-Seine, France). Another text, prepared by Dr Thomas Oden (Drew University, NJ, USA), gathered representative materials from previous dialogue documents on the themes of religious liberty and proselytism. This and a number of brief theses reflecting on this material, prepared by Rev. John Haughey, S.J., were discussed as well. Those participating in the meeting were well satisfied with their progress in clarifying some of the important theological and related practical issues affecting relations between the two bodies. But it was evident there was more work to be done on these topics at the next meeting, the final one in the current series, which was set to occur in a year's time.

Ecclesiology at Kuala Lumpur 2001

The mini-consultation prior to the 2001 General Assembly arranged by the Executive Director was held 2-3 May, 2001 on the subject of ecclesiology, to coincide with the Assembly theme. It was a loosely organized event, more in the nature of round-table with a flexible program than a normal consultation with plenary and group work arranged on a formal timetable. About twenty people attended various sessions, some of whom were new to the TC; their presence provided a fresh and hopeful dynamic, especially those who had connections with NEFs and other significant theological bodies in their home areas. Seven papers were presented, several of which were later published in ERT,[89] and a valuable brainstorming session gathered ideas for TC work from participants at the consultation.

In addition to the mini-consultation, the TC conducted several sessions in the Assembly program. Two of them were joint sessions with the Commission on Women's Concerns (CWC), in which they launched books and papers and made a highly significant statement on the problem of the abuse of women.[90]

---

[89] Papers from the TC Consultation and the Assembly appeared in ERT 25:4 (Oct 2001); 26:1 (Jan 2002); 26:2 (April 2002), 27:1 (Jan 2003).

[90] These sessions featured Mrs Lynn Smith, Dr Catherine Clark Kroeger and Dr Nancy Nason-Clark for CWC and Dr T. Oden for the TC. The volume *No Place for Abuse* (Downers Grove: InterVarsity, 2001) by Kroeger and Nason-Clark was also launched.

Chapter VI Networking Theologians

There were also two open sessions conducted by the TC, the first explaining its work and seeking to attract interest from Assembly participants. Dr Ken Gnanakan spoke about his interest in environmental stewardship and announced details of a study project on the topic, which gained several responses. The other session was a seminar on globalisation led by Dr Donald Tinder (Tyndale Seminary, Amsterdam and the Evangelical Theological Faculty in Louvain, Belgium). All four of these sessions were well attended and generated considerable sympathy and support for the TC.

Director concludes

The General Assembly signalled the end of a term for the TC and its Executive. However, there was no general meeting because the membership system was now defunct since it had not been followed up from the last general meeting in 1996. Only three of the seven members of the Executive appointed at that time were still active; they, with other invited guests, discussed business between consultation presentations and other sessions.[91]

The starting point was the confirmation of the role and vision of the TC previously developed in Tuebingen in 1998, and finalised in Vancouver in 2000. This saw the TC as a global network with a central representative core group carrying the focus of the work, supported by specific study units, task forces and publications. The most serious business, however, was the financial situation which was now extremely critical due to the large expense associated with salary payments and the CD-ROM project.

It was obvious to all that the TC was in an extremely difficult position. After much consideration it was decided that Dr Stamoolis would conclude his service as Executive Director forthwith, after three years in the position. There were also implications in this situation for relationships between the TC and the WEF organization, but they were not resolved, not least because the WEF itself was entering on a period of organizational uncertainty at the same time. Of necessity, therefore, Dr Rolf Hille resumed his previous dual role of Executive Chair and various aspects of

---

[91] Attended by the three official members, R. Hille (Chair), K. Gnanakan (Vice-Chair) and D. Parker (Editor) along with J. Stamoolis, Executive Director. An apology was received from W. Gasque whose involvement in the Executive concluded with this session. G. Vandervelde (convenor Ecumenical Issues), D. Hilborn (UK) and B.J. Nicholls were present as guests.

the work would be shared among the remaining members. Dr George Vandervelde (Canada, convenor of the Ecumenical Task Force) and Dr David Hilborn (Director of the UK Evangelical Alliance Theological Commission) were added to the Executive, making five in all, with approaches to other potential members to be made as soon as possible.

One element of the program which was deliberately retained was the long running series of talks with the Roman Catholic Church which were now expected to come to a conclusion in sessions set for early in 2002. The Orthodox dialogue mooted for many years was now not likely to occur for the present time due to Dr Stamoolis' departure. The Environmental stewardship study initiated earlier by Dr Ken Gnanakan was also endorsed again.

Chapter VII A New Role for a New Century

Regrouping amidst setbacks

At the end of this decisive TC meeting, re-grouping was starting to take effect, providing good hope for future. Plans for the following year's program, a joint consultation with the Fellowship of European Evangelical Theologians (FEET), were endorsed and preliminary plans were laid for the program for the following year.

Later in 2001, Dr David Parker visited Korea to promote the work of the TC during participation in theological consultations there. He also represented the TC at the General Assembly of the ATA in Kuala Lumpur when Dr Ken Gnanakan concluded twenty years' leadership of that body. At the biennial meeting of the South Pacific Association of Bible Colleges, Dr Parker discussed the proposal to hold a joint conference in 2003, but this plan to extend the TC's policy of shared fellowship and consultation did not materialise.

One other positive sign towards the end of the year was the publication of the book, *Hope Does Not Disappoint*, by the Eschatology Study Unit from the 1996 London consultation, headed by Dr Jochen Eber, then of Chrischona Seminary, Basel, Switzerland. This was conceived as a textbook on the model of the successful Carson Faith and Church Study Unit volumes, and accessible to a wide range of readers, especially students beginning their theological studies. It featured sixteen writers from all continents.[92]

In late 2001, as the constructive initiatives from the Kuala Lumpur meeting were beginning to be implemented, the most serious problem of all occurred. The WEF was in the process of a radical restructuring following reports at its recent General Assembly of a critical financial situation and the end of Jun Vencer's term as International Director. Because of its deficit arising from the unexpected salary payments and the unrecouped costs of the CD-ROM project, TC finances were frozen by the WEA leadership, suspending most operations. Only generous special private funding by long term friends of the TC prevented a complete close down, including the publications.

---

[92] Jochen Eber (editor), *Hope Does Not Disappoint: Studies in Eschatology - Essays from different contexts* (Bangalore: TBT, 2001 and published in Germany by Verlag fuer Kultur und Wissenschaft.

In this unexpected and critical context it was even suggested by one senior WEA leader that the TC should change from being a WEA Commission to become an independent body with affiliate status. The idea of expanding into an international evangelical theological association had been under consideration by the TC leadership already for some time, but it was finally concluded that the advantages such an arrangement might bring would be outweighed by the need for the WEA to support a theological commission and for the TC to serve the WEA constituency as it had done since its inception. However this idea would soon come back onto the agenda.

Considerable discussion took place in the ensuing months to clarify misunderstandings about where responsibility lay for funding of the CD project and salary payments. As a result, the suspension of TC finances was lifted in mid-2002, enabling its operations to resume. However, finances were still severely restricted requiring tight controls on all expenditure.

The WEF also made progress with its own restructuring, appointing a Secretary-General as the chief administrator. The appointee, who took up the position from July 2002, was Gary L. Edmonds, who had previously served with the development organization, Interdev; he had also been a pastor in USA and European director of Christian Associates International. He set up his office in Seattle, USA, and the other WEF offices in Singapore and Wheaton were closed. The name of the organization, now representing over one million local churches in 110 nations, was also changed to 'World Evangelical Alliance' (WEA) to better represent its intention to operate as a cooperative body harnessing the efforts of its various constituent agencies.

The financial crisis severely affected planning for the final session of the decade-long WEF/Roman Catholic talks, due to be held only a short time later. With considerable sacrifice on the part of the TC participants, they were held on schedule at Swanwick, England, 17-26 February, 2002. Significant changes had taken place in both sponsoring bodies in the time between the previous meeting and this one. Three new participants on the WEA side attended for the first time: Dr Rolf Hille (TC Chairman), Dr David Hilborn (Theological Advisor to the Evangelical Alliance UK), and Rev. Carlos Rodríguez Mansur (Fraternidad Teológica Latinoamericana in Brazil). The Consultation had before it an integrated draft of a proposed common report, and aimed at bringing it to a completed form. The text achieved at the end of the week included two main parts. Part I focused on convergences between Catholics and Evangelicals on *koinonia*; and Part II on the relationship of *koinonia* to evangelization.

It was agreed that the completed report would be presented to the sponsoring bodies requesting approval for its publication as a 'study document' in the hope that it could be 'widely discussed.' It was stressed that it was 'not an authoritative declaration' of either of sponsoring bodies, both of which themselves would 'evaluate' it. The completion of this text brought this phase of conversations to a close. As they finalised the session, the participants expressed the hope that this consultation between the World Evangelical Alliance and the Catholic Church would continue.

Global perspective in Germany 2002

One strand in the TC's new strategy was to hold conferences in cooperation with other theological groups. The first of these was a joint conference with FEET at Woelmersen, Germany in 16-20 August, 2002. About one hundred people, including the regular FEET participants and members of the TC, focused on the theme, 'European Theology in World Perspective,' featuring speakers from Europe and many areas of the developing world. Most of the papers from this highly successful venture were published in ERT,[93] and the positive experience confirmed the value of the strategy.

The value of the conference was further enhanced by the fact that ICETE also held its Executive meeting at the same site prior to the main conference and some participants stayed on to share in it. This allowed some consolidation of the relationships between the two bodies which had been re-affirmed at the October 2001 meeting. The TC agreed that its next cooperative conference would be with ICETE in 2003.

Moving on

The annual TC Executive meeting which took place 20-22 August, 2002, following the TC/FEET conference, was of crucial importance. It presented the first opportunity to make a definite start to the process of rebuilding the TC in the new environment it faced, now that the financial and personnel crises which had dogged it so continuously in recent years were apparently in the past. However, the financial settlement with WEF left the TC in a difficult position, which made the organization even more grateful to the ELCW for its continued faithful support.

The Executive meeting was attended by the TC members plus several guests, but the WEF leadership was not represented. The new structure of

---

[93] See ERT 27:3 (July 2003); 27:4 (Oct 2003).

a working core group was formally endorsed, thus officially ending the old arrangement of a larger membership panel, and terminating the uncertainty about the status of those who had been slated for membership in 1996. Dr Brian Edgar (Australia) and Dr Tom Oden (USA) were added to the new core group which now constituted the TC membership. Other names, especially from Africa, Latin America and Asia, would be added as soon as possible to complete the global perspective.

A program of activities was also adopted, contingent on finance and personnel, which included study units, publications, dialogues and a 'rapid response task force.' It was decided that large scale conferences should be held in conjunction with future WEA Assemblies.

One further area of development taken up was renewed cooperation with the Lausanne movement, especially in its Forum on World Evangelization planned for Pattaya, Thailand in October 2004. Dr Hille had accepted an invitation to become co-chair of the LCWE's Theology Working Group in the spirit of the new vision for the TC which had been forged at its Vancouver meeting two years earlier, calling for it to make 'strategic alliances with organizations that share our goals and objectives.' The Executive made a number of suggestions about the Forum program and built official participation in the Forum into the TC program for 2004.

There was also endorsement of various initiatives in the area of TC publications, including *ERT*, *TN* and electronic publishing. Dr George Vandervelde was appointed as convenor of dialogues, a position which would include both the existing talks with the Roman Catholic Church (then approaching a critical point) and others that were under consideration.

Although it was recognised that many of these initiatives were of a long term nature and that the financial basis of TC was still critical, the meetings ended on a buoyant and positive note. As an act of faith, a process was even established for the appointment of a new Executive Director. Members felt that major steps had been taken to re-establish the TC, and that the future would soon see the fruit born of the years of difficulty. The next meeting was set to coincide with the ICETE consultation exactly a year ahead, in which TC members would also participate.

Less than a month after this decisive session, there was another significant development from the WEA. The International Council announced that it had appointed its Secretary-General, Gary Edmonds, as acting Executive Director of the TC. Although Edmonds already had an onerous and demanding responsibility in guiding the WEA as it restructured and re-financed itself, Dr Hille was hopeful that this surprising new development would be advantageous for the work of TC and also ease the

Chapter VII A New Role for a New Century 95

heavy administrative load which he carried in addition to his work as head of an important theological institution in Germany. He envisaged that the Secretary-General would be of great assistance in relations with the WEA, and especially in the crucial area of fund-raising.

Dr Hille's own role now would be caring for the business sessions, co-ordinating the joint conferences, maintaining contact with theologians around the world (including the recruitment of additional participants in the TC program), and contributing to the publications. It was also hoped that individual members of the TC could take specific responsibility for various aspects of the program, perhaps on an honorarium basis. However, the practical details of the new arrangement would need to be worked out in discussions between Hille and Edmonds in ensuing months.

During the year further developments in the renewed growth of the TC took place. At the invitation of Dr Hille, Dr Wilson Chow (Hong Kong) re-joined the TC after a break of ten years. Dr Hille travelled twice to Asia and Pacific, visiting seminaries and making contact with individuals and local evangelical fellowships to promote the work of the TC; he also shared in planning for the LCWE Pattaya Forum 2004. Working with Dr Hilborn there was also progress on the revision of the revision of the WEA statement of faith. As Director of Publications, Dr Parker continued with *ERT* and *TN*, and also arranged to bring the CD-ROM (which had sold out) back into limited production, and to update its contents.

Expansion in 2003

Although there had been some uncertainty about the way the TC would operate in the light of the unexpected action of the WEF International Council in appointing an acting Executive Director, expectations were high for the 2003 meeting of the TC to be held in conjunction with the ICETE consultation, 18-22 August. Originally planned for Kiev, Ukraine, the venue was changed to the Wycliffe Centre near High Wycombe, UK for practical reasons. It attracted a capacity crowd of more than 150, and featured a quality program, with some high profile international speakers; the theme centred on paradigm shifts in global tertiary education and their implications for theological education.[94]

---

[94] ICETE adopted a new mission statement at these meetings: 'The mission of ICETE is to promote excellence and renewal in evangelical theological education worldwide by cultivating community and facilitating collaboration among its constituent associations and related entities.'

Almost all of the TC members attended the Executive meeting held prior to the consultation. In addition, there were two theologians from the Korea Evangelical Theological Society (KETS) in attendance by invitation with a view to the appointment of one of their nominees to the TC. Subsequently, Dr Jae Sung Kim, of Hapdong Theological Seminary, was added to the TC membership, bringing the total to eight, with vacancies for representatives from Africa and Latin America to be filled as soon as possible. With the addition of Dr Kim, half of the TC membership was now directly related to national fellowships and theological associations, in line with the policy which aimed to make the world body representative of its global constituency.

For the first time in many years, the WEF leadership was represented at a TC meeting in the person of the Secretary General, Gary Edmonds, whose contribution facilitated discussion, especially on matters concerning relations between the TC and WEA. Being more familiar now with the work of the TC, he was happy to relinquish his role as interim Executive Director. Concrete plans for the future were developed, focusing first on the involvement in the LCWE Pattaya Forum in 2004, followed by a joint-consultation and meeting in Korea with the KETS in 2005, leading to a full scale consultation the following year.

There was a positive report on progress with Dr Ken Gnanakan's Environment Stewardship study project, which was authorised for publication. It was also decided to develop a unit, coordinated by Dr David Hilborn, to provide the WEF with brief statements on urgent theological issues facing the global evangelical constituency. Ken Gnanakan was also authorised to work with Gary Edmonds in developing ideas on large scale projects dealing with major theological and related issues such as HIV/AIDS, pluralism, family and gender, which would integrate with the activities of other WEF Commissions and agencies. Initial ideas for another task force on Jewish evangelism were also endorsed.

The possibility of further ecumenical talks were reviewed, although progress stalled on the publication of the final report of the talks with the Roman Catholic Church due to the uncertainties which arose at the May 2003 WEA International Council meeting. The papers were published a short time later in two Roman Catholic periodicals.[95]

A major centre of attention was the involvement of TC members in a joint track with ICETE personnel during the subsequent Consultation on

---

[95] Pontifical Council for Promoting Christian Unity (PCPCU) *Information Service*, N. 113 2003/II/III, pp. 85-101; *Origins* (Conference of Catholic Bishops in the U.S.) 16 Oct 2003 Vol. 33, No. 19, pp. 310-320.

the theological basis for theological education. In a three day program, several present and former TC members helped create the groundwork for an ongoing task force of TC and ICETE members to develop one of the themes of the ICETE 'Manifesto' which called for a 'theological grounding' for theological education. Papers from this group were planned for publication in 2005 as the basis for the further development of the evangelical theological education globally, especially through ICETE and TC networks.[96]

On the organizational side, it was decided to appoint Dr David Parker as Director of Administration (in addition to his work with publications), thus relieving Dr Hille of much of the day to day work and making it easier for him to continue his role as Executive Chair.

Thirty years

Following the High Wycombe meeting, Ken Gnanakan worked on his environmental book; he also prepared submissions on the integrated study projects and an assignment on the family initiated by WEA Secretary-General Gary Edmonds. David Hilborn and George Vandervelde developed plans for publications arising out of the work of the Ecumenical Issues Task Force, while initial ideas on the Jewish evangelism task force began to take shape. David Parker visited South Africa to represent the TC at a conference on HIV/AIDS, and took the opportunity to meet with key evangelical leaders there and in Singapore. In mid-2004, he carried out the same function in Seoul, Korea while attending other meetings. Several TC members became actively involved in preparation for the Lausanne Forum on World Evangelisation to be held in Pattaya, Thailand in October 2004; there was also planning for the joint-meeting with the Lausanne Theology Working Group to be held prior to the Forum.

However, the TC was thrust into uncertainty once more when, in February 2004, the WEA Executive announced a plan to carry forward its ongoing process of restructuring to a further stage. One of the main elements of this plan was to do away with commissions by changing them into independent bodies known as 'affiliates' which would be only loosely connected to the WEA. For the TC, this suddenly brought back into view the possibility of creating an 'international evangelical theological society' to link theologians and institutions around the world. This idea had

---

[96] Dr Brian Edgar, Dr David Hilborn for the TC and Dr Larry McKinney for ICETE were appointed to head this project.

been considered quite seriously a few years before, only to be rejected. However, in this new context it became a critical option.

But as the year progressed, the pressure for urgent change eased as the proposals for the WEA restructure were gradually moderated. By the time of the 2004 TC meeting, held at Bangkok in September, there was a determination to push ahead as positively as possible with the policies and plans that had been taking shape in recent times. Most critical to this decision was the guidance offered by WEA International Council Vice-Chair, Rev. Wong Kim Kong of Malaysia, who represented the WEA during an lengthy and productive session of the Bangkok meeting.

To facilitate this progressive approach, the membership of the TC was further enlarged. Dr Carver Yu, of China Graduate School of Theology, Hong Kong was appointed to replace his colleague, Dr Wilson Chow; additions were Rev. Per Pedersen of the Danish Mission in Armenia and Dr Claus Schwambach, Faculdade Luterana de Teologia, São Bento do Sul, Brazil. Definite ideas were discussed to fill the remaining vacancies.

Dr Ken Gnanakan's environmental stewardship book[97] was launched and plans adopted for broad distribution to maximise its value as a study text and tool for action. It was reported that the up-dated CD ROM had been selling well, and the new administration system based at the Brisbane office was bedding down effectively. Steps were taken to refine and expand the constitutional aspects of the Commission, and to expand its categories of memberships so that a wider range of people and institutions could participate in its work.

Ideas for literary projects were also ventilated, with the news that the joint project with the ICETE on the theology of theological education was on target for publication in mid-2005. Approval was given to publish the papers from the final talks with the Roman Catholic Church in February 2002.[98] Plans for promotion of activities and for future meetings were refined, especially the joint conference with KETS in Seoul in late 2005. Substantial work was done on the revision of the WEA statement of faith, which was scheduled for finalisation in a year's time after further wide consultation.

The joint meeting with the LCWE Theology Working Group showed how much there was in common between the two bodies, especially a desire to network effectively, although their differences still meant that merger was not feasible. This kind of global fellowship with its promise of

---

[97] Ken Gnanakan, *Responsible Stewardship of God's Creation* (Bangalore: WEA Theological Commission/Theological Book Trust, 2004).
[98] ERT 29:2 (April 2005).

further development was an appropriate prelude to the highly productive involvement of TC members in the Lausanne 2004 Forum on World Evangelization which was held immediately afterwards at Pattaya, Thailand.

Chapter VIII Reaching the Goal 2005-09

Renewed hopes in 2005

With the TC now 30 years old, there was a quite different context from the time when it had been founded. There was a significant increase in the number of well resourced seminaries in the majority world, and many more people from these areas had received a high quality theological education.

This new context provided the TC with a greatly increased scope for networking theologians and theological institutions around the world, and the diversity that existed made the task all the more important. Although there were pressures on the TC itself, the decisions made at the 2004 annual meeting provided a good foundation for it to fulfil its vital role. Consequently there began a surge which continued for several years.

There were additional members and new study initiatives such as Ken Gnanakan's work on the environment and Brian Edgar's on biotheology and public theology. Edgar had also taken responsibility for cooperation with ICETE on the theology of theological education project; the papers from this effort were published in ERT July 2005. David Hilborn had already begun working on a review of the WEA statement of faith in association with a similar project for the UK EA; he was also looking at attitudes to other faiths. Dialogues with the Roman Catholic Church were under the leadership of George Vandervelde, and there was hope that a similar move could be made with the Orthodox now that Per Pedersen who was working in Armenia was part of the group.

The TC's prospects were improved with a change of leadership in WEA. In February, 2005, Gary Edmonds resigned as Secretary-General after less than three years in the post. This opened up the possibility of a full scale review of WEA operations. Geoff Tunnicliffe was appointed acting leader and a top level 'strategic summit' involving all arms of the WEA was held in May 2005 in Orlando Florida. The TC was represented at this event, where the first edition of this book was launched along with Ken Gnanakan's study on environmental stewardship as well. The plans for a new approach to WEA activity matured at this Orlando meeting. There was further progress in this direction at a meeting of international leaders held in December in Israel. This allowed the TC as with other commissions to plan more firmly and to work together more cooperatively in the overall mission of the WEA.

The core executive group was a key factor in the progress of the TC. However, the size and representation of this group was limited by the long-standing policy of the TC that members would chosen on the basis of their suitability according to agreed criteria and were to be funded by the TC as needed, rather than being composed simply by those were had the opportunity and means to attend. Because of pressures on the TC budget, this meant that not all regions of the world could be yet be represented. There was hope that some sympathetic groups might be interested to assist; FEET, for example, showed interest in helping to sponsor a member from Africa to enable that important area to be represented. Another scheme under consideration was a system of 'extended membership' which would see the possibility of individuals, and representatives of national TC and seminaries contributing their own involvement without putting additional pressure on the TC budget.

Meanwhile, a four part plan for the annual meeting of the TC was being developed which would produce effective results. Each annual session would feature the normal meeting in which the TC core members would transact their business, but in addition there would be other elements – a mini-consultation on a topic of global importance, a symposium on a topic of local importance, and finally, fellowship with local theologians and ministry in local churches where possible. Cooperation would always be sought with any theological association and seminaries in the host city.

Seoul Korea 2005

This plan worked well for the annual gathering held in September 2005 in Seoul, South Korea, where TC member Dr Jae Sung Kim was a key leader in Korea Evangelical Theological Society. This long standing and active group was instrumental in organising a successful consultation on 'The Task of Evangelical Theology for the Church of the 21st Century' at the Sungkyul University. TC members also visited a number of seminaries, not only in the capital but elsewhere in the country as well.

The business session was able to make considerable progress, updating the TC By-laws in the wake of the developments at WEA level, especially by instituting the new category of extended membership (later known as the Global Membership Scheme). This system would enable national and regional theological commissions, seminaries and individuals to be members of the TC and to be able to contribute to the work of the organising by attend meetings at their own expense and to receive in return copies of the TC journal and newsletter and be connected with other theologians on a regular basis. This scheme proved to be exceptionally beneficial in future years, but meanwhile the TC was looking at ways to fill gaps on its core membership, especially from Africa and Latin America.

Plans were also developed for new task forces to study Jewish evangelism and Integral Mission. There were also plans for new developments in ecumenical discussion, although there was still resistance in some WEA circles to the dialogue with the Roman Catholic Church; these difficulties needed to be resolved before further progress could take place. A project which had been remitted to the TC some years earlier was finalised when it was decided that the revised EA UK statement of faith should be recommended to the WEA for adoption. Dr David Hilborn had been working with both the EA UK and the TC on this project.

Another important step was underway as well with news of the revival of the Lausanne Theology Working Group under the leadership of former TC member, Dr Chris Wright with the prospect of another global conference on evangelisation in view. The TC offered support for this development and anticipated opportunities for cooperation between the two groups.

Theological conferences

With these positive steps, it seemed that the plans that had been developing for some time might at last be within reach! The momentum continued into the next year.

Earlier hopes that the TC might be able conduct a significant event in conjunction with the 9th WCC Assembly at Porto Alegre, Brazil in February 2006 (as it had done in Canberra, 1991) did not eventuate. However, the TC was represented by David Hilborn, along with WEA International Director, Geoff Tunnicliffe as official observers.

In August 2006, Carver Yu represented the TC at the biennial consultation of ICETE at Chiang Mai, Thailand where he was one of the featured speakers. At about the same time, Dr Rolf Hille was in Prague, Czech Republic, leading a group representing the WEA in the first session of discussions with the Seventh-day Adventist Church. This event aimed at establishing points in common between the two groups and clarifying misunderstandings with a view to possible cooperation. A second round of talks was held a year later at Andrews University, in Berrien Springs, Michigan, USA. The findings, released in a statement issued at the close of discussion, indicated that there could be much closer relationships between the two traditions, and also the possibility of Adventist membership in the Evangelical Alliances.

Meanwhile, honorary member of the TC, Thomas Oden, was developing his new Early African Christianity project which had arisen out of his Ancient Christian Commentary series and sought to give recognition to the significant part played by Christianity in this part of the world. This project was linked to TC and provided a backdrop for the annual meeting of the September 2006, which was held for the first time ever in Africa. Some of the key early leaders of the TC had come from Africa but there had been no significant meeting of the organisation in that continent.

Kenya 2006

The venue was NEGST (now the School of Theology of Africa International University), an important seminary in Nairobi, Kenya and facilitated by James Nkansah-Obrempong, Professor of Theology at NEGST. It followed the new pattern with a consultation on 21 September on 'Religious Fundamentalism as a Global Issue'. Keynote speakers were Dr Yusufu Turaki (Nigeria/Kenya) and TC chair, Dr Rolf Hille.[99] This successful event was followed the next day by a symposium on African theology covering topics such as Christology, hermeneutics and comparisons between Christian and Islamic approaches to Scripture. Each of these events attracted about 30 participants.

A pastoral statement issued from the fundamentalism consultation was widely distributed and well received, while the opportunity for local theological college students and faculty to attended the symposium was warmly appreciated. TC members also met with leaders of the Association of Evangelicals of Africa and the Kenya Evangelical Alliance; some of them preached in local churches at the weekend.

In addition to these main events, there was a parallel workshop held elsewhere in the city on HIV/AIDS, led by Ken Gnanakan and Professor Danny McCain of Nigeria with the assistance of World Vision (Kenya). An action plan to assist churches was prepared and expectation of further developments in the future.[100]

During the business sessions a notable contribution was made by members of the extended membership scheme which had been launched at the beginning of the year. In particular, a proposal by Matt Cook (La

---

[99] TN 35:4 (October 2006) p 1, 2 (statement); the papers were published in ERT 37:2 (April 2007).
[100] TN 36:2 (April 2007), p 2.

Faculté de Théologie Evangélique de l'Alliance Chrétienne, FATAEC, in Abidjan, Cote d'Ivoire) arising out of his paper to the symposium for a task force on contextual exegesis was firmly adopted and was due to produce fruitful results in later years.

The growth of the TC was now positive enough for some long anticipated changes to take place in its leadership. Dr Hille indicated that after 20 years involvement with the TC (half of them as Executive Chair), he was wanting to hand over the leadership to a new generation in the next year. Dr Ken Gnanakan also indicated that he was ready to do the same. Dr David Hilborn (EA UK) who had been anticipated to succeed Dr Hille regretfully announced that a change in his employment meant that it would not be possible for him to continue with the TC. Dr Hille was therefore reappointed as Executive Chairman but a firm decision was made to seek a replacement within the year. Dr David Parker's appointment as Director of Administration and Publication was extended by two years to July 2009 with the intention also of finding a replacement by then or sooner.

Dr George Vandervelde's appointment to the TC was also extended by two years so that he could continue to lead the ecumenical dialogue activities which were at a delicate stage with a decision about the publication of documents from the last round of talks with the Roman Catholic Church soon to be made. It was hoped that an understudy for this important and critical ministry could be found.

Although there were still difficulties to be overcome, the historic session of the TC in Kenya concluded on a positive note.

TWG and other conferences

In February 2007 some members of the TC, including David Parker, Michael Glerup and Matthew Cook, returned to Kenya for a consultation sponsored jointly by the TC and the revived Lausanne Theological Working Group and held at Limuru near Nairobi. This was an exploratory conference, meeting under the theme, 'Following Christ in a Broken World', to test the feasibility of a conducting a series of consultations to provide comprehensive and detailed theological input for the proposed third Lausanne conference on evangelisation. This event was expected to be held in 2010, to coordinate with the celebration of the centenary of the famous Edinburgh World Missionary Conference.

The Kenya conference was organised by Chris Wright and attracted about 30 participants. Papers were presented covering the wide range of topics. As a result of the discussion, it was decided that there should be three more conferences, one each year until the major Lausanne event. The initial papers were published in *ERT* October 2007, and the TWG arranged for 5000 extra copies to be printed for wide distribution amongst its own constituency and elsewhere.

Meanwhile, the TC task forces and other study projects gathered pace. Ken Gnanakan continued work on the HIV/AIDS project, while Matt Cook's contextual theology group made positive plans for production of their papers and the publication of a book. Similarly, a team of scholars with particular experience and background were preparing for the study on Jewish evangelism, with the organisational assistance of the evangelistic organisation, Jews for Jesus; this was seen as a necessary follow-up to the earlier Willowbank consultation.[101]

There had been some progress on the dialogue with the Roman Catholic Church which had been stalled due to resistance by some of the WEA constituency to such discussions. Following on submissions made by the TC from its 2006 meeting, the WEA IC had decided that the dialogue could be continued with the understanding that the papers were to be considered as study documents rather than official statements. The WEA participants were also to include evangelicals from Catholic dominated countries (but, in any case, these conditions were no problem as the TC had always adopted these policies in the past). The sudden death on 19 January 2007 of the TC convenor, Dr George Vandervelde, who had led the dialogue activity for many years, soon after these decisions were made created difficulties for their implementation, but Dr Rolf Hille was ready to take over and head up the process.

Concerted efforts were made to encourage theological commissions and associations in countries around the world to link themselves with the TC through the Extended Membership scheme, now in its second year. David Parker visited as many as he could on his travels and information, including Guide Sheets on how to form and operate a Commission, was sent to many national EAs which had not yet formed a group. As a result, there was a steady increase in membership from national bodies as well as individuals and seminaries.

Philadelphia 2007

The major event for 2007 was the annual gathering which was held in Philadelphia, USA. On his return from Israel where the annual WEA leaders' meeting had been held, David Parker visited the area in December

---

[101] See above at Note 46.

Chapter VIII Reaching the Goal 2005-09

2006 and confirmed the suitability of the area. With the assistance of Dr Chris Hall (Eastern University) and Dr Jae Sung Kim, now a pastor of a Korean church in the city, the program was developed.

The major component was a consultation on 31 July at Palmer Seminary where Dr Ronald Sider, a former leading member of the TC, was the well known Professor of Theology, and president of Evangelicals for Social Action; he had also been recently appointed by the WEA to head its newly formed initiative on global civic engagement. Papers on the topic, 'Providence and Political Involvement' were presented by Dr Sider and Dr Claus Schwambach of Brazil; they were followed by a discussion period led by Dr Brian Edgar resulting in the drafting of a carefully worded 'Philadelphia Statement' on 'Evangelical Social Engagement.'

The symposium was held at Westminster Seminary focusing on 'Theology and Ministry' with addresses by Dr Peter Lillback, President of the seminary, and Dr Dennis Cheek from the Ewing Marion Kauffman Foundation.

Previous planning came a positive climax at the business sessions conducted during the gathering when several changes and additions were made to the membership and leadership of the TC. Dr Rolf Hille had led the TC in the dual role of Executive Chairman for most of the time since 1996 and was anxious to hand over to a younger person. Dr Brian Edgar, who had been the leader of the Australian Evangelical Alliance theology unit, had been seriously considering the suggestion that he should succeed Dr Hille. However, Dr Edgar had recently taken up a new academic post with Asbury Seminary, USA and was not sure if he would be able to do justice to the TC chairmanship in his new role. So he agreed to become Vice-Chairman with a view to taking on the position in October 2008 when it was hoped that a new leadership team would be finalised within the framework of a 5 year strategic plan.

Dr Hille retained the position of chairman and Dr David Parker was appointed Executive Director (part time) (cutting short his earlier appointment by a year – 2009 back to 2008). At this meeting, Dr Ken Gnanakan (India) stepped down from the position of Vice-Chairman, ending more than 20 years of involvement with the TC. Dr David Hilborn, who had been head of Theology for the UK Evangelical Alliance for several years, stepped down in 2006 due to a change in his employment, and was replaced on the TC by Dr Justin Thacker, his successor in UK.

Dr James Nkansah who had played such a strong role in organising the 2006 annual gathering in Kenya was appointed a member of the TC, thus filling a long standing vacancy for African representation. Dr Chris

Hall was also appointed as a North American representative to replace the late Dr George Vandervelde.

Ideas were discussed to fill the remaining regional vacancies on the TC, but its work was strengthened by the active participation once again of several Extended Members representing national TCs and other bodies. It was hoped that soon Dr Edgar would feel able to take over the leadership role from Dr Hille and that a new full-time funded Executive Director could also be found. However, some of the discussions indicated that these plans might not work out smoothly.

For the first time, Geoff Tunnicliffe, International Director of WEA, was present at a TC meeting and he presented a document in the process of finalisation detailing the relationships between the WEA and its Commissions. Clarification of these arrangements was well overdue, and the document generated vigorous discussion, especially when Dr Edgar pointed out the anomaly that it contained. Commissions were answerable to the WEA and existed to further its cause, but they received no funding from the WEA. Dr Edgar pointed out the contradiction of this, and compared it with the situation that existed in the national alliance in which he had worked where the commissions were fully funded by the parent body.

Funding had been a critical issue for the TC, especially in recent years, and it was disappointing that in the new era of the WEA, there would be no relief. In fact, the TC had found that even in its day to day management of finances, WEA rulings created difficulties and imposed extra unnecessary costs and delays. Despite this, there was no possibility of the WEA changing its policy on the funding of its commissions; the arrangements were cemented when the document was finalised later in the year. This decision set in train a sequence of events that was have considerable significance for the TC.

The TC was present again for the WEA ILT held in Kenya in November 2007 where planning for the GA to be held late in 2008 was high on the agenda. Some WEA members also participated in the Global Christian Forum which followed. This new ecumenical gathering was meant to draw in the evangelical and pentecostal churches around the world in a way that the conciliar movement had not been able to do. The focus was on individual participation and the sharing of testimonies of faith.

After the success of TC gathering in Africa in 2006, it was planned to expand the TC's activities to another area of the world that had been neglected for so long – Latin America. Some of the early prominent leaders of TC had come from this area and developments there at the time had been a major focus of TC interest. However, as with Africa, it had not been possible in recent years to include this region in the TC's activities. This was all the more critical because of the rapid growth of evangelicalism in the region. A start had been made by the appointment of Dr Claus Schwambach of Brazil to the TC in 2004, and it was hoped that there could be the appointment of a Spanish speaking representative soon.

Accordingly, plans were being prepared for a meeting of the TC in the region in 2008, but the announcement by WEA that it would hold a GA in Thailand in 2008 meant those plans had to be delayed. In any case, whenever the meeting could be held, a lot of work was needed to make up lost ground and to reconnect with the evangelical theological institutions there and their people.

Thanks to a generous gift from a Hong Kong donor, it became possible for David Parker as Executive Director to make an extensive tour of Latin America in April-May 2008. His visit, which was facilitated in Brazil by Dr Claus Schwambach, covered Chile, several areas of Brazil, Argentina, Peru and Guatemala. Valuable contacts were made, and many opportunities opened to lecture, preach and promote the work of the TC.

A particular feature of the visit was meeting with some of the 'old lions'[102] of the TC who had made such a notable contribution in earlier times, including Rene Padilla (Argentina), Pedro Arana (Peru), and Emilio Nunez (Guatemala). There was also effective contact with AETAL (the association of Bible schools), Latin American Theological Fraternity and several other organisation, seminaries, universities. Inspections were made of sites that could be suitable for a consultation, ideas about a relevant program were ventilated and potential additional members of the TC were identified.

The reception was encouraging, but the need for definite action was reinforced when the most disconcerting question of all was asked, 'Why have we not had a visit from the anyone in the TC before?'

Lausanne Theological Working Group

The first of the three planned consultations on the Lausanne theme took place in February 2008 at Chiang Mai, Thailand with the topic, 'The Whole Gospel'. About 30 theologians were present, many of them with connections to Langham organisation; David Parker and Justin Thacker represented the TC. The next consultation was held at Panama in January 2009 with Rolf Hille and Justin Thacker representing the TC where the

---

[102] For the reference to 'old lions' see Samuel Cueva, 'Missionary Theology in Context: Marks of Mission from CLADE V' (ERT 38:1 (Jan 2014), 54-69

theme was 'The Whole Church'. The final gathering focused on 'The Whole World' was in February 2010 at Beirut.[103]

The overall result of this intensive series conferences was an impressive body of papers which would provide a comprehensive theological foundation for participants at the Cape Town 2010 event. Already many extra copies of ERT featuring the papers had been distributed globally and there plans for a statements from the conferences to be circulated as well. There had also been other input from the conferences such as specific suggestions for the program; as head of the TWG, Dr Chris Wright also had direct input into the planning for the event.[104] Chris Wright, who was one of the major speakers at Cape Town, took the main responsibility for organising the TWG conferences but the TC was an active partner.

Productive program

The TC's own program in 2008 was also a productive one, but difficulties were also encountered which had serious ramifications. The major event would be the annual gathering in Thailand and participation in the GA.

Earlier in the year preliminary meetings for next round of dialogues with the RC Church were held 26 Feb 2008 in Rome. The Center for Early African Christianity developed its program with its first International Consultation in Ethiopia 11-12 April 2008. Then in August the two task forces brought their work to a climax. The contextual exegesis group led by Matt Cook held a concentrated writing session at Wycliffe Hall Oxford to finalise papers ready for publication. At about the same time, the Uniqueness of Jesus and Jewish Evangelism group held its consultation at Woltersdorf near Berlin, preparing its papers and issuing a statement which was widely circulated.

In his travels in Asia, Europe and Africa, the Executive Director made good contact with national TCs, theological associations and seminaries. The Global Membership scheme continued to expand steadily.

Bangkok 2008

The annual gathering for 2008 was planned for Bangkok to be followed by the GA at Pattaya. There was high expectation that this event would see further consolidation and progress. The usual multi-pronged program

---

[103] Papers from the LTWG sessions appeared in ERT 33:1 (Jan 2009); 34:1 (Jan 2010); 34:3 (July 2010)
[104] TN 38:4 (Oct 2009), p 3.

had to be modified because of the WEA GA being held immediately after the TC meeting. There would only be opportunity for a modest consultation involving local theologians and some informal fellowship.

The consultation was held at the Baptist Seminary on 24 October on the theme, 'The Holistic Gospel in a Developing Society.' There was a wide range of local theologians and guests in attendance to hear papers by James Nkansah (Kenya) and Justin Thacker (UK), to join in small group discussion of several key aspects of the theme, and for fellowship over a shared meal. A statement was prepared for publication.[105] The consultation was held in conjunction with the inaugural meeting of the Fellowship of Theological Institutes of Thailand

Business was dominated by a sudden change in TC leadership. It was expected that Dr Brian Edgar would take over the role of chairman as planned in 2007. However, the concerns that he had expressed at that time about the organisational relationship between the TC and the WEA had escalated. In June 2008, WEA International Director, Geoff Tunnicliffe, had visited Australia and there had been intensive discussion between him and Dr Edgar on the issue. Dr Edgar had not been convinced and, being unwilling to commit himself to working as chairman of a commission in such an arrangement, he withdrew his agreement to become chair and also withdrew from membership in the Commission.

Therefore, when the TC met in Bangkok, it was necessary to re-think its leadership planning. Dr Hille was no longer available to continue as chair so Dr Thacker of UK was appointed acting-chair with Dr James Nkansah as vice-chair. Dr Justin Thacker, who had joined the TC in 2007, was a medical doctor with specialisation in paediatrics and had served for some time in Africa. He studied at London School of Theology and gained a PhD from King's College London. He was currently head of theology at EA UK, having succeeded David Hilborn in that post. Dr David Parker's appointment as Executive Director was extended to 2009, but if no replacement had been found by then, it would be extended again for another year.

The membership of the TC core group was extended with the appointment of Rev. David Roldan as a representative of Spanish speaking Latin America. He already had a fine record of scholarship, pastoral concern and administrative leadership as Dean of Facultad Internacional de Educacion Teologica (FIET), Buenos Aires, Argentina, editor of a theological journal and a former National Secretary of the Accreditation Associa-

---

[105] The papers are accessible at http://www.worldevangelicals.org/commissions/tc/PDF%20(TC).pdf).

tion of Seminaries. His appointment brought the representation from Latin America up to full strength. There was also discussion on the possibility of appointing a suitably qualified theologian from the WEA Women's Commission to redress the gender balance of the TC.

The Berlin statement on Jewish evangelism was endorsed and consideration was given to possible new projects now that the existing ones were coming to their successful conclusion.

After the end of the TC meeting, several members attended the WEA 12th GA at Pattaya. There was little formal involvement by the commissions at this event, but the TC display stand attracted favourable attention. It was supplemented by a range of material from Oden's Early African Christianity project.

The sudden change in leadership prospects at Bangkok was disappointing, but there were other positive developments so the TC ended the year planning on forging ahead with its program, especially the much anticipated consultation in Brazil in 2009.

In 2009 Dr Rolf Hille was appointed as ecumenical relations spokesperson for the WEA, which meant that responsibility for the dialogues would officially pass from the TC to the WEA itself, but the TC resolved to maintain good informal relations with Dr Hille in this important area of work. Meanwhile, Dr Hille was making preparation for the first session of the new round of the talks with the Roman Catholic Church scheduled to be held in association with the TC gathering in Brazil later in the year.

With new younger leadership hopefully in the place soon, together with the filling of the remaining vacancies, it was hoped that there could be considerable growth in the next few years even though the budget was likely to be affected by gloomy world financial situation. After Latin America, there were possibilities of holding consultations with annual gatherings in southern Europe or the Middle East in 2010 and in West Africa in 2011. There would also be the finale of the TWG conferences and active participation in Lausanne III. There was talk also of linking up with other theological societies and expanding the publications more widely by electronic means , and the possibility of a new relationship with the Lausanne TWG.

Publications

Meanwhile, publications continued to be a significant part of the TC program. Books from the contextual theology and the Jewish evangelism projects were under way, but would take some time to appear. The quarterly *Theological News* was still produced regularly, with more the 700 copies being posted to seminaries, individuals, and the WEA family in all parts of the world; the entire run of back issues from 1969 to 2004 was available for purchase on a CD. There was also an electronic version emailed twice each quarter and a regular update for Global Members, all of which helped promote the TC activities and invite helpful responses. The CD of *ERT* and other TC publications was due to be updated with more recent material[106]. However, a sudden steep increase in cost while this move was being actioned meant that the update did not go ahead.

There was considerable concern about the journal, *Evangelical Review of Theology*. There was a regular supply of articles and reviews which were the responsibility of the TC, but difficulties were beginning to develop with the production of the journal.

From the beginning of the journal in 1977, the generosity and vision of Jeremy Mudditt, Managing Director of Paternoster Press had been a significant factor in its success, but his health problems in the late 1980s meant that Paternoster Press became part of Send the Light (STL), a large Christian literature distribution agency, which had originally been associated with Operation Mobilisation; it later merged with the International Bible Society (now Biblica) to create a huge global business. Paternoster periodicals, including ERT, were part of the Authentic Media division of STL with Jeremy Mudditt as Publishing Manager. From 1995, further health problems meant that Jeremy Mudditt became a consultant to STL, but was still heavily involved, and remained highly supportive of ERT.

However, in 2008 the global financial crisis and difficulties with a new computer system combined to cause severe difficulties for STL's operations in the UK. One of many steps that it wanted to take was to cease production of its journals. Not wanting to see this happen, Jeremy Mudditt succeeded in arranging for AlphaGrahics, a company in Nottingham which had already been producing a lot of Paternoster materials, to take over the management; *ERT* was one of only four journals that AG considered viable.

So from January 2009, *ERT* was produced by AlphaGraphics with the TC continuing to provide content as before. However, there were considerable logistical difficulties in making the transfer, and the first two issues of 2009 were delayed considerably. This was an embarrassment to the TC because one of those was a special TWG issue which was needed

---

[106] Additional material included the extra volumes of *ERT* up to 2005 (Vol 29), and 3 books, *Responsible Stewardship of God's Creation* by Ken Gnanakan, *Hope does not Disappoint* —textbook on eschatology edited by Jochen Eber, and *Discerning the Obedience of Faith: A short history of the WEA Theological Commission* by David Parker.

for the continuing series of conferences; problems with this issue were also aggravated by difficulties in TWG supplying art work. One positive development from the transfer to new production arrangements was the availability of on-line subscriptions; electronic versions of *ERT* were also available but not at any discounted pricing.

There were more difficulties for *ERT* when Jeremy Mudditt's wife, Mag, became seriously ill thus curtailing Jeremy's involvement; she died late in 2009, only to be followed by his own illness, and then his death a short time later on 21 April 2010. Meanwhile, the business prospects of STL deteriorated even further, going into administration in December 2009 and being liquidated a year later. Parts of the company were sold off in December 2009 with Authentic Media (including Paternoster) being acquired by the Australian book distributor, Koorong which purchased its intellectual property, contracts and other parts of the business. However, these developments had no direct impact on *ERT* because the 'Paternoster periodicals' continued to be produced by AlphaGraphics in Nottingham as a virtually separate operation.[107]

In the early part of 2009, the TC was involved with some other conferences. The TWG took place in Panama City, in late January with the theme, 'The whole church,' again involving about 25 participants from 12 countries, including Dr Rolf Hille, Dr Justin Thacker and Dr Daniel Salinas (Paraguay) for the TC.

In Africa, Matt Cook was the TC representative at a conference on 'The future of Evangelical theology in Francophone Africa' held in Bangui, Central African Republic, May 17-21, 2009. At this event, funded by the Overseas Council and others, the need for contextual theology along the same lines as the TC's own project was fully recognized. Further information about Lausanne III in Cape Town was expected mid-year after a conference of leaders in Seoul, South Korea.

However, the major event for 2009 was the long awaited consultation in Brazil, but before this a major change took place.

Change in leadership

Soon after the 2008 meeting in Bangkok, following discussion with UK EA, it was confirmed that Justin Thacker would be able to take over as chairman of the TC. He would have no trouble maintaining his regular work as head of theology for EA UK as well as fulfilling his role with the TC be-

---

[107] AlphaGraphics Nottingham was sold in 2014 to AlphaGraphics Stockton on Tees but no changes in day to day operations were anticipated.

cause the TC chairmanship was an honorary position which was mainly concerned with the annual meeting and the general operation of the TC as a committee and not the day to day work of the TC or its contacts with the WEA. This contrasted with the position of Executive Director, however, which was normally full time, appointed by and answerable to the WEA ID; also unlike the chairmanship, the position of Executive Director was officially recognised in the WEA organisational structure.

However a few weeks later, early in the following year, Dr Thacker began to seek ways in which he could secure funding to enable him work part-time as both Chairman and Executive Director. In anticipation of this development, he started to take active control and to involve himself in the day to day affairs of the TC.

This meant that the activities of the current Executive Director were restricted and so in April 2009, Dr David Parker indicated to the WEA ID that he would be concluding his work would hand over all operations to Dr Thacker. Dr Parker's involvement with the TC, which first began in 1986, ended on 30 June 2009. Old records were sent to the Billy Graham Centre Archives which housed other TC and WEA material, while current records were sent to London.

Dr Thacker now took over all the normal administrative activities, editorial work on ERT, *TN* and the website, the Global membership scheme, relationships with the WEA and other outside bodies; in particular, he was responsible for planning of the annual gathering and consultation in Brazil.

One of the new developments was the immediate cessation of the production of *Theological News* as a printed publication because it was considered to be expensive and outmoded as a form of communication. It was planned instead to commence a website with varied content with which theologians around the world could interact.

Sao Paulo, Brazil 2009

The 2009 annual gathering was held as planned in Sao Paulo, Brazil, 22-25 July, consisting of the annual business meeting and a symposium for theologians of the region. Attendance by global members was smaller than usual.

A major concern for the business session was Dr Thacker's role in the TC. He was still officially the chairman only, but after discussion it was agreed that the TC would recommend to the WEA that he be appointed Executive Director for a period of 5 years. Under this scheme, the TC would provide funding to the EA UK to cover 30% of his time, while EA UK would provide additional funding, so that he could devote 50% of his time to TC work; Thacker would remain as an employee of the British body rather than the TC or WEA.

Another important part of the business session was to reassess the vision and purpose of the TC in the light of the recent changes to its leadership and to plan for the future. The representation of various parts of the world on the TC core group was also a matter for discussion. The meeting was told that there were now many networks of theologians and institutions which had not existed in earlier times, and that there was now no longer any need for the TC to focus on developing these kinds of groups. Instead it should be more focused on the global situation and in providing theological insights relevant to the serious issues facing the church in the world. One way of expressing this new direction, it was decided, was to have *ERT* concentrate more on thematic issues in the future.

In what the chairman said was a 'turning point' for the TC[108] the meeting developed a new vision statement to state what was unique about the TC, deciding on the slogan: 'Providing theological reflection from a global perspective.' In other words,

> In faithfulness to Christ and in order to serve the Church, the Theological Commission of the World Evangelical Alliance exists to provide international theological reflection on issues of importance affecting the church and society everywhere.

Therefore the TC would aim 'to be a prophetic evangelical voice that is globally representative, faithful to Scripture, theologically informed and which speaks with clarity and relevance to both the church and the world.'

These new goals would be carried out by representative teams of expert theologians addressing major issues, working in partnership with other groups as appropriate and disseminating their findings as widely and effectively as possible. It would also encourage others groups and individuals to do the same.

The consultation was attended by about 80 participants, mostly from Brazil, and dealt with the state and nature of contemporary evangelical theology in Latin America. Main addresses were given by Ricardo Barbosa, Daniel Salinas and Marcelo Vargas, while other significant contributions came from TC members Claus Schwambach, David Roldan and

---

[108] *TN* 338:4 (December 2009), p 1.

James Nkansah with Valdir Steuernagel and Norberto Saracco also presenting addresses.[109]

A wide range of issues was raised by the papers and discussion, such as fragmentation of evangelicalism, the visibility of public witness, and a lack of an explicit systematic theology. There was also concern expressed about the responsibility for keeping alive an evangelical spirit faithful to the 1974 Lausanne tradition, and the way in which the evangelical movement should relate to neo-pentecostalism. Overall there was a major focus on maintaining the legacy of the evangelical tradition, especially as linked to the pioneers of Latin American evangelical theology.

Chairman's resignation

There was little follow up to implement the new 'vision' for TC adopted at this meeting in the remainder of the year, and even the regular activities declined; there was little involvement by the core or global members. *ERT* continued to be produced but *TN* did not appear in either print or electronic form. However, the TC was represented by Dr Thomas Schirrmacher and Dr Rolf Hille at a conference held in Bad Urach, Germany in September 2009 on the theology of suffering jointly sponsored with the WEA Religious Liberty and Missions Commissions and the Lausanne Theology Working Group; the statement and papers from this consultation were published in *Suffering, Persecution and Martyrdom – Theological Reflections* edited by Christof Sauer and Richard Howell.[110] The final Lausanne TWG conference took place in Beirut, Lebanon 14-19 February 2010 with the topic, 'The whole world', although without formal TC representation; the papers were published in the July 2010 issue of *Evangelical Review of Theology*.

There was unexpected and serious development when in February 2010, when overnight, Dr Thacker resigned from his position with EA UK for personal and family reasons; as a consequence, he was also obliged to resign from his role with the TC. None of the arrangements which had been made at the last annual TC meeting in Brazil for Dr Thacker to share his time between the EA UK and the TC had ever been formalised and he had not been formally appointed as Executive Director.

---

[109] Some of the papers were published in *ERT* 34:4 (Oct 2010).
[110] Bonn: VKW, 2010 (Religious Freedom Series Vol 2); see also *Bad Urach Statement* edited by Christof Sauer (WEA Global Issues Series Vol 9 Bonn: 2012).

Chapter IX Re-Building – An Integrated Unit 2010-2014

Restoration and new leadership

To deal with the emergency created by the sudden vacancy in the leadership and administration of the TC, the International Council, with the full recommendation of the International Director, appointed Dr Thomas Schirrmacher of Bonn, Germany, at very short notice as Executive Chairman. Dr Schirrmacher, a prominent German evangelical scholar and religious liberty activist, was well known in WEA circles through his involvement in the IIRF, as spokesman for Human Rights and in ecumenical discussions. He had also been active in regional and national theological associations including FEET and ATA, as well as lecturing at various seminaries and conferences around the world. Since 1996, he was the Rector of the multi-campus international Martin Bucer Seminary, based in Bonn.

Even though Dr Schirrmacher had not been a member of the TC before, he was quite familiar with its earlier ethos and aims, and with the wider WEA family. After quick consideration, Dr Schirrmacher agreed to accept the appointment, with the determination to do what he could to restore the TC, although, by necessity, it would be a rather different kind of operation for the immediate future at least. His immediate brief was to make the TC a part of the day to day operation of the WEA.

He faced a daunting task – not only did he already have many existing responsibilities, but the suddenness of the transition meant that there was no opportunity for the normal smooth transfer of information and records. In addition, many contacts had been lost, much of the activity that had been built up over the previous few years had been wound down in the previous months and the proposed website for *Theological News* had not functioned. These difficulties were exacerbated because Dr Thacker had concentrated all of the main functions of the TC into his own office, but he also had extensive responsibility for his role with the EA UK which severely limited the time he was able to give to the TC.

One of the most pressing issues was the production of ERT. An issue of *ERT* featuring papers from the recent final session of the TWG conference was due to be finalised very soon after Dr Thacker's resignation. Dr Schirrmacher turned to Dr David Parker and asked him to assist with the role of 'Executive Editor' working with Dr Schirrmacher as General Editor. Due to a misunderstanding, Chris Wright and the paper writers from the TWG were not aware that their material was required so quickly. However, with the failure of the recent change of ERT editorial policy to attract contributions for a highly focused thematic series, there was no other material available. So some quick work by contributors and the new Executive Editor, together with a short postponement of the copy deadline, saw the issue to the press in good time.

There was a similar problem with *TN* which had been suspended as a printed publication for almost a year. Dr Schirrmacher decided that it should be restarted as a valuable means of reporting and promoting the activities of the TC. Dr Parker was invited to take on responsibility for this project as well. Over the next few months, all the missing back issues were made up (although one was a combined number) and regular publication resumed. However, it was distributed as an electronic version, emailed and downloadable from the website, rather than in printed form posted to the large number of recipients as previously

One of the first issues of TN, dated July 2010, carried a statement by Dr Schirrmacher outlining the current situation and future plans for the TC. He pointed out that there had been many changes in the people involved in the TC, but that with the publications in hand, efforts could continue to re-build. The existing TC web site had been updated with information about these developments.

Dr Schirrmacher's announcement also stated that one of his main responsibilities as chair had been 'to visit high ranking leaders of non-Evangelical churches [and] to give them a fair presentation of our views over a lot of prejudices around and to assure friendship for times of common need.' Another major aim had been 'to ensure that whenever theological consultations take place on an international level, we take part and present our case. We have been involved in some of these events recently, and we are now building up a list and network of people who can represent us.' One such occasion was the World Mission Conference in Edinburgh, Scotland 2010, and another would be the Third Lausanne Congress in Cape Town later in the year.

Taking the evangelical voice to other groups and presenting the evangelical case at conferences constituted a new mode of operation for the TC which contrasted with its traditional role as a network of theologians. Another important function also received greater emphasis – assisting the WEA in the preparation of statements which required theological insight. Dr Schirrmacher was much in demand as a speaker and travelled widely, often dovetailing his new TC role with his other commitments in religious freedom and as an evangelical spokesman in his own region.

The core membership of the TC had been reduced significantly in the previous year with the departure of several of its key leaders, although Vice-Chair, Dr James Nkansah, Kenya, remained in his position. However, it was still anticipated that a regular meeting could be held in 2010, as planned, at the Lausanne Cape Town conference. Dr Schirrmacher contacted the remaining members in the hope that many of them would be at the conference and it would be a simple matter to conduct at least a short meeting. While many were expected to be at the conference in some capacity, it was soon found that it would be virtually impossible to organise a meeting due to the difficult logistics and security considerations. Plans for the meeting were therefore abandoned, and it was hoped that there could be one held sometime in early 2011. However, this never eventuated and the membership dispersed. The Global Membership scheme was not maintained either.

TC at Cape Town 2010

Many of TC members were at the Cape Town conference, including Dr Rolf Hille; Dr Carver Yu was one of the featured speakers[111] who made a presentation on the truth of the gospel. Dr Schirrmacher spoke at some ancillary gatherings, met many friends of the TC and distributed quantities of TC literature and CDs from a large display booth. He also conducted a workshop on the code of ethics for mission and spoke at the assembly of the WEA Mission Commission. Dr Rosalee Velloso Ewell of Brazil, who had strong links with TWG and Langham ministries, was on the statement committee. The TC acted as theological consultant to the WEA in its role as a co-sponsor of the conference, advising on the drafting and endorsement of the documents. A meeting of the WEA International Leadership Team was also held, involving the TC.

A major anticipated outcome of the Cape Town event was a much closer relationship between the WEA and the Lausanne Movement. There was a feeling that there ought not to be two global evangelical bodies vying for the attention and support of the evangelical constituency. The two groups had worked together closely in the lead up to Cape Town with WEA being recognized as working in 'collaboration' with the LCWE for this event – although the lead was always taken strongly by the LCWE. The cooperation between the theological groups of WEA and LCWE was

---

[111] See report *TN* 39:4 (November 2010) p 2.

stronger, so there was much anticipation that the groups might merge or at least continue to work closely together after Cape Town.

All this meant that plans for the growth and re-development of the TC would need to take into account the possibility of an entirely new set of arrangements in which the TC would be joined by LCWE personnel. Therefore there was some hesitation in restoring the activities and organisation of TC to their former states, with the expectation that further changes would soon be necessary.

Executive Director appointed

However, towards the end of the 2010, it was becoming clear that without an active membership and staff, the burden of maintaining the work of the TC in its current form, let alone restoring it to its earlier method of operation or planning for a new context, was a heavy responsibility for the chairman alone. So attention was turned to securing assistance. The efforts which had taken place so far to keep the core of the TC functional had provided assurance of continued financial support which meant that appointing a new Executive Director was the best way to go; filling this position was one of the priorities that the WEA International Director has assigned Dr Schirrmacher at the beginning. By December, Dr Schirrmacher had written to the members stating that he was recommending Dr Rosalee Velloso Ewell for the post;

Dr Velloso Ewell, a daughter of pastor, was a Baptist theologian from Brazil, who gained her PhD at Duke University (USA) and for the previous 7 years had been Professor of New Testament Theology and Ethics at the South American Theological Seminary in Londrina, Brazil. She currently served as New Testament editor for the *Latin American Bible Commentary* project, and was a member of the Lausanne Theology Working Group. She was expecting to move to UK early in 2011 where her husband would be engaged in doctoral studies. If approved, Dr Velloso Ewell's appointment, as a theologian from the Global South, would be a good balance for Dr Schirrmacher.

TC members gave their tacit approval and the appointment was made by the WEA International Council in November 2010; however, an announcement was delayed until April 2011 to allow time for re-settlement in UK. Dr Schirrmacher said, 'I have already had the chance to work together with Rosalee on WEA projects as well as in discussions with the Vatican in Rome, the World Council of Churches in Geneva and other international conferences. I am convinced that we have made a good choice. Rosalee is deeply convinced of Evangelical values, but open to

Chapter IX Re-Building – An Integrated Unit 2010-2014   123

learn from others. She has a clear stand point where needed, but is open to work together with the wide range of the Evangelical family.'

In a further winding back of the changes discussed in 2009, he advised that the new Executive Director's 'first task will be to connect to as many as possible of the theological commissions of national and regional alliances, or to the alliances themselves, where there is no network of theologians as of yet.'

By now it was also clear that the mooted changes to the TC work due to a merger with LCWE would not materialise because, during further discussions, it became apparent that there was little, if any chance, of progress on this plan. It soon became bogged down in uncertainty about the role and distinctive ethos of the two parent organisations and the practicalities of how such a relationship could be made to work organisationally. At the level of the theological groups themselves, there was even less prospect because the TWG lacked strong leadership after Chris Wright, who had so expertly guided its activities in the build-up to Cape Town, withdrew from any further involvement so that he could give his attention to his work with Langham Ministries.

The future for the TC was also becoming more assured because of developments within the WEA. During the latter part of 2010, the WEA organisation was clarifying the role of commissions and their chairs, a process that affected all commissions but particularly TC because of Dr Schirrmacher's dual role as Executive Chairman.

Progress for the new-look TC

So although there was considerable clarification of the context in which the TC would operate in the immediate future, hopes of further meetings of the core membership receded. Carver Yu resigned his membership in November 2010 because of dissatisfaction with the process by which the Executive Director was appointed, due in large part to difficulties in communication at the time.

Dr Velloso Ewell took up her new role as Executive Director more fully and worked with the Chairman by writing and publishing papers. The two leaders participated extensively in conferences and meeting with key leaders, which was an important means by which the TC took up the 2009 vision of dealing with the big global issues. Their activities covered a wide range of topics. They participated for example in the development of a code of ethics for mission which involved both the Vatican and the World Council of Churches; this was launched in June 2011 at the WCC headquarters as 'Christian Witness in a Multi-Religious World: Recommendations for Conduct.' In 2012 Dr Velloso Ewell presented this code to the Baptist World Alliance in her role on the Baptist-Muslim relations task force of the Freedom and Justice Commission; this role also saw her in the Nigeria giving lectures and workshops.

Another important project was the statement, Evangelism: The Hallmark of Evangelical Faith which was incorporated in the address by the WEA Secretary General, Dr Geoff Tunnicliffe, at the Vatican Synod of Bishops in October 2012. Dr Schirrmacher attended this Synod and was also present at then inauguration of the new pope in 2013.

Both Dr Schirrmacher and Dr Velloso Ewell participated in the Global Christian Forum, Manado, Indonesia in October 2011. They were together again for the WCC General Assembly in Busan, South Korea in October 2013. The two TC leaders were regular visitors to consultations of the groups like ICETE, FEET, ATA and the Micah Challenge, as well as meetings of other WEA commissions. They participated in the Evangelical-Orthodox dialogue which took place in 2013 in Tirana. Dr Velloso Ewell gave many lectures to theological associations including the Scottish Evangelical Theological Society, while Dr Schirrmacher made presentations at the 2011 gathering on Theological Education by Extension in Kathmandu, Nepal.

Nearly two years after his appointment as Chair, following a WEA Leadership meeting, Dr Schirrmacher was able to report that he and Dr Velloso Ewell had made considerable progress in restoring the work of TC, despite the wind down in membership and older activities. There had been many discussions with former TC personnel and with leaders of seminaries and associations which had links with the TC in the past, while visits to conferences and the regular meetings of some of these groups opened the way for further cooperation and interest.

The regular publications, ERT and TN continued to appear and the two books from the task forces finally appeared.[112] There were also plans for further development including a new website with weekly commentary and a news blog, a series of small publications on 'Global Issues' to be circulated electronically, and the re-establishment of the Global Membership scheme. It was also anticipated that there would be plans for consultations, and for working together with other WEA commissions.

The three key personnel, Dr Schirrmacher, Dr Velloso Ewell and Dr Parker met in mid-2011 and again in 2013 to discuss publication and oth-

---

[112] *Local Theology for the Global Church* (William Carey Library) was published in 2010; *Jesus, Salvation and the Jewish People* was published in 2011 by Paternoster despite its parent company undergoing many financial and corporate issues.

Chapter IX Re-Building – An Integrated Unit 2010-2014   125

er plans. Some 'Senior Advisors' were also appointed including Dr Chris Wright, Dr Bruce Nicholls, Dr Thomas K. Johnson and Dr Ken Gnanakan.

So while the TC was operative during this period, the earlier pattern of a core membership facilitating the development of a global network of evangelical theologians and institutions had not been restored. Instead, the new mode was more like the pattern that had been called for much earlier – the TC was a small unit operating within the WEA structure representing it on various platforms, and providing advice on theological matters. The sudden changes of 2010 had provided the opportunity for this pattern to be implemented although it had been rejected by the TC at the time. The other alternative presented then, for the TC to become virtually an independent international theological society only loosely connected to the WEA, had been never been totally dismissed.

Although the new form of the TC was gradually consolidating, there was still much more that could be done. There was an addition to the 'Global Issues' series[113] and in 2013 the 'World of Theology' series was launched. The TC had also successfully cooperated with the Missions Commission and the Religious Liberty Commission in another publication, *Sorrow & Blood: Christian Mission in Contexts of Suffering, Persecution, and Martyrdom*, with chapters by 62 authors from 23 countries. This book was launched on 27 September 2012 by WEA Secretary General, Dr Geoff Tunnicliffe, at the Religious Freedom Roundtable in Washington D.C. and the first copy was given to Scott Felipe, Deputy Director for Policy and Research at the United States Commission on International Religious Freedom (USCIRF).[114]

The new web site was still not operative, and there were issues confronting the TC's flagship publication, ERT. Rapid changes in print publishing of academic journals meant higher subscription costs and lower circulation, leading the publisher, AlphaGraphics to consider a much improved web-site for their journals. However, this would involve considerable amounts of extra work by the TC which it was not well place to supply and for which there would be little return; the TC continued to supply all the material for *ERT* without any charge, but it was the publisher who received the financial returns! Furthermore, there was a smaller contact pool, due to the loss of the previously extensive mailing lists and dimin-

---

[113] *Racism* by Thomas Schirrmacher with an essay on Caste in India by Richard Howell was published in 2012 as volume 8 of the 'Global Issues Series'; this series had commenced in 2008 under the general umbrella of the World Evangelical Alliance and the International Institute for Religious Freedom (IIRF).

[114] It has its own website: http://www.sorrowandblood.com/

ished relationships with theologians and societies across the world, which meant that the supply of material for both ERT and TN was sometimes critical.

Another of the TC's success stories had also been impacted due to changes in technology and the fortunes of the TC. With the change in leadership and staffing of the TC, it was no longer possible to manage retail sales of the *Theological Resource Library* CD which had produced good revenue for the organisation over several years. So from 2010 it became a wholesale operation only. Then in June 2011 Logos Bible Software who produced the CD announced that, in response to general trends in the industry, it would change to on-line delivery only; the TC would continue to receive the royalties on sales, but these proved to be much lower than under the previous arrangement.

In the wider evangelical world, there were many developments and activities such as the 40th anniversary of ATA (which was an original project of TC), the appointment of a theological leader in Africa, Langham Ministries' establishment in Francophone Africa, and the regular conferences of ICETE. The TC kept in touch with many of these bodies and was often invited to be present at and participate in many of their activities.

Preparations were being made for another round of dialogues with Roman Catholic Church, led by Dr Rolf Hille. After the initial preparatory meeting at the Vatican in 2008, the first discussion session was held in Sao Paulo, Brazil from 26 July to 1 August, 2009. The focus was on convergences between Catholics and Evangelicals on doctrinal matters and contemporary ethical issues. The second meeting was held 12-17 September, 2011 at the Vatican, with close attention paid to scripture and tradition in the life and mission of the church, with attention to the particular ways in which each side understood these authorities. Wheaton, Illinois, was the venue for the third round the next year where soteriology was central topic; many of the differences had been already overcome by the 'Joint Declaration on Justification', which was worked out between the Pontifical Council for Promoting Christian Unity and the Lutheran World Federation. However, the role of the Church was not discussed in this context, and therefore this question was still open in the ecumenical context.

The next round of discussions were held in Guatemala City 1-7 September 2013, where surveys conducted by both Catholics and Evangelicals were used to examine how religious minorities were treated. The aim was to encourage a more mature expression of religious freedom on the part of the leadership of the two groups in areas where tension had often been apparent; the question of collaboration was also under discussion.

The final session in this series is due in September 2014 in Bad Blankenburg, Germany where the papers and statements will be finalised for publication.

WEA participants included Dr Rolf Hille (Germany) as convenor, Dr Leonardo de Chirico (Italy), Rev José de Segovia Barrón (Spain), Dr Jeol C. Elowsky (USA), Dr Timoteo D. Gener (Phillipines), Dr James Nkansah-Obrempong (Kenya) and Dr Claus Schwambach (Brazil), with Dr Solomo Strauss (Germany) as a regular guest.

Forty Years of Witness

Since its official formation in 1974 (with a pre-history going back to 1968), the TC has been through many phases. It has established a good record in sponsoring conferences, encouraging TCs and associations, creating a fellowship of theologians, operating a scholarship fund, publishing books, journals and newsletters. Over the years it has been able to voice evangelical concerns and be a bellwether on crucial issues, speaking on its own behalf or in cooperation with others. During all this time, it kept firmly in mind the aims of its founders – developing national theological commissions and regional associations and strengthening evangelical theological education.

At its peak, it involved 50 or more members from all parts of the world, and at other times, it was effectively linked with many national and regional theological groups, seminaries and individuals, all contributing to its goal of 'promoting biblical truth by networking theologians.' However, recent changes have seen the organisation transformed into a small working unit integrated into the structure of the WEA, providing theological insights and presenting the evangelical perspective on a wide range of issues in many different forums on behalf of its mother organisation.

As it marks 40 years of witness, the context is vastly different from the days of its origins, and many problems remain. However, there is still a need for a unit such as the TC to be, as the proposed Vision Statement of 2009 put it, 'a prophetic evangelical voice that is globally representative, faithful to Scripture, theologically informed and which speaks with clarity and relevance to both the church and the world.'

APPENDICES

Appendix A

Vision Statement

THE THEOLOGICAL COMMISSION OF THE WORLD EVANGELICAL FELLOWSHIP/ALLIANCE
(Adopted Vancouver, 2000)

PROMOTING BIBLICAL TRUTH BY NETWORKING THEOLOGIANS

The Theological Commission of the World Evangelical Fellowship exists to promote biblical truth by networking theologians to serve the church in obedience to Christ.

1) By internationalizing theological frameworks.
2) By encouraging original theological reflection and research.
3) By defending and confirming the gospel.
4) By focusing discussion on practical and relevant themes in varied contexts.
5) By articulating biblical truth in forms accessible to all Christians.

THIS WILL BE ACCOMPLISHED BY

1) Networking evangelical theological organizations and theologians worldwide.
2) Organizing theological reflection teams, task forces, study groups, dialogue groups and other international gatherings.
3) Disseminating theological reflection about biblical truth in clear and concise formats for use at by the church at all levels.

TO MEET THESE OBJECTIVES THE TC WILL

1) Establish effective communicative networks of theologians, educators and church leaders.
2) Partner with regional and national Evangelical Fellowships of Theologians to sponsor joint conferences, plan joint publications and foster exchange of theological educators.

3) Partner with other organizations that are involved in theological education, dissemination of literature and student scholarship programs.
4) Form strategic alliances with organizations that share our goals and objectives.
5) Mobilize volunteers, part-time staff and recruit other full-time staff to work toward agreed goals.
6) Engage in a vigorous program of research and publications of topics that apply biblical understanding to relevant problems facing the churches in their ministry.

Appendix B

Theological Commission Fact Sheet
Theological Assistance Program (TAP) – established 1968
Theological Commission – established 1974

CHAIRMEN OF THE EXECUTIVE COMMITTEE
Dr Byang Kato 1975
Dr Arthur Climenhaga 1975-1980
Dr David Gitari 1980-1986
Dr Peter Kuzmic 1986-1996
Dr Rolf Hille 1996-2008
Dr Justin Thacker 2008-2010
Dr Thomas Schirrmacher 2010-

EXECUTIVE SECRETARIES / DIRECTORS
Dr Bruce J. Nicholls 1969-1986
Dr Sunand Sumithra (1986-89)
Dr Bong Rin Ro 1990-1996 (acting 1989-1990) on furlough 1995-1996
Dr James J. Stamoolis 1998-2001
Dr David Parker 2007-2009
Dr Rosalee Velloso Ewell, 2010-

ADMINISTRATORS
Dr David Parker 1995-6, 2003-2007
Dr Rolf Hille 1996-98, 2001-2003

GENERAL MEETINGS AND CONSULTATIONS
1975 September: London, 'Defending and Confirming the Gospel'
1978 January: Willowbank, Bermuda (with LCWE), Consultation on Gospel and Culture
1980 March: Mabledon, Kent
1980 March: High Leigh, UK (with LCWE), International Consultation on Simple Life-style
1982 June: Grand Rapids, Michigan, USA (with LCWE), Consultation on the Relationship between Evangelism and Social Responsibility
1983 June: Wheaton 'The Nature and Mission of the Church'

1985 May: Oslo, Norway (with LCWE) Consultation on the Work of the Holy Spirit and Evangelization
1986 June-July: Singapore 'Jesus Christ our Redeemer and Liberator'
1988 January: Hong Kong (with LCWE), 'Conversion and World Evangelization'
1989 April: Willowbank, Bermuda, 'The Gospel and Jewish People'
1990 June: Wheaton 'Theological Issues in the 90s'
1991 July: London (with ICAA), 'From Text to Context in Theological Education'
1992 June: Manila, Philippines 'The Unique Christ in our Pluralistic World'
1993 October: New Delhi, India, Consultation on the 'Evangelization of the Poor'
1996 April: London, 'Faith and Hope for the Future'
2001 May: Kuala Lumpur (in conjunction with WEF 11th General Assembly), Ecclesiology
2002 August: Woelmersen, Germany (joint with FEET), 'European Theology in World Perspective'
2003 August: High Wycombe, UK (joint track with ICETE), 'Theology of Theological Education'
2004 Sept-Oct: Bangkok, Thailand, including Joint Sessions with LCWE Theology Working Group and Issue Groups of LCWE 2004 Forum on World Evangelization
2005 September: Seoul, South Korea (with Korea Evangelical Theological Society), 'The Task of Evangelical Theology for the 21st Century'
2006 Sept: Nairobi, Kenya, 'Religious Fundamentalism as a Global Issue'; 'African Theology'
2007 July-August: Philadelphia, USA, 'Providence and Political Involvement'; 'Theology and Ministry'
2008 October: Bangkok, Thailand, 'The Holistic Gospel in a Developing Society'
2009 July: Sao Paulo, Brazil, 'Evangelical Theology and Evangelical Movement in Latin America'

JOINT CONSULTATIONS WITH LAUSANNE THEOLOGY WORKING GROUP, IN PREPARATION FOR CAPE TOWN 2010

2007 February: Limuru, Kenya, 'Following Christ in a Broken World'
2008 February: Chiang Mai, Thailand, 'The Whole Gospel'.
2009 January: Panama City, Panama, 'The Whole Church'.
2010 February: Beirut, Lebanon, 'The Whole World'

PERIODICALS

Theological News first published 1969 – merged with Theological Education Today 1982-90; Changed to electronic PDF form 2010

Evangelical Review of Theology – first published 1977: Editors – Dr B.J. Nicholls 1977-86, 1991-98; Dr S. Sumithra 1986-1990 Dr Bong Rin Ro 1990; Dr D. Parker, 1999-2009; Dr J. Thacker, 2009; Dr T. Schirrmacher & Dr D. Parker, 2010-

Transformation first published by TC January 1984 (until July 1988) Editors – Dr Tokunboh Adeyemo, Dr Ronald Sider, Rev. Vinay Samuel.

ORGANIZATIONS

International Council of Accrediting Agencies (ICAA): established 1980 (name changed to International Council for Evangelical Theological Education, ICETE, 1996)

Faculty Development Scholarship Scheme: 1979-1996

STATEMENTS ISSUED BY THE WEA THEOLOGICAL COMMISSION FROM CONSULTATIONS:

2005: Church, Evangelization, and the Bonds of Koinonia: A Report of the International Consultation between the Catholic Church and the World Evangelical Alliance (1993—2002)

2006: HIV and AIDS – Response and Action. Nairobi, Kenya

2006: Pastoral Statement on Fundamentalism. Nairobi, Kenya

2007: A Statement on Evangelical Social Engagement. Philadelphia, USA

2007: WEA/Adventist Statement

2008: Statement from the Theological Commission Consultation on Holistic Ministry: Bangkok, Thailand

2008: The Berlin Declaration on the Uniqueness of Christ and Jewish Evangelism in Europe Today

CAPE TOWN COMMITMENT, 2010

The WEA Theological Commission was involved in writing, editing and approving the Cape Town Commitment – available on-line at http://www.lausanne.org/en/documents/ctcommitment.html

TC Publications

NEWSLETTERS
WEF Theological News (1969+) (on-line version from March 2002) (also available on CD, 2005)
Programming (ceased publication)
Theological Education Today (ceased publication)
Evangelical Review of Theology (1977+)
Transformation (published by TC 1984-88)

ELECTRONIC TEXTS:
WEF/WEA TC Theological Resource Library CD (Amsterdam edition, 2000; v 1.0, 2000; v2.0 2004; v 3.0, 2006 – previously available as a CD but now for on-line download direct from Logos Bible Software)
WEA Theological News CD 1969-2004 (2005)

OCCASIONAL PAPERS – 'ISSUES AND IDENTITY' SERIES
Karl Barth's Theology of Mission, by Waldron Scott, 1978
The Biblical Doctrine of Regeneration, by Helmut Burkhardt, 1978
Contextualization: A Theology of Gospel and Culture, by Bruce J. Nicholls, 1979
Evangelicals and Social Ethics, by Klaus Bockmuehl, 1979
Pornography: A Christian Critique, by John H. Court, 1980
Theology and the Third World Church, by J. Andrew Kirk, 1983
The Unique Christ in our Pluralistic World (WEF TC Manila Declaration, 1992)
An Evangelical response to 'Confessing the one Faith' (WEF TC Ecumenical Issues Task Force, 1992)
Evangelical Christianity and the Environment (WEF TC Ethics and Society Study Unit and Au Sable Institute Consultation, 1992)
Toward a Theology of Theological Education, by Dieumeme Noelliste (ICAA Consultation, 1993)
Sharing the Good News with the Poor (1993 WEF TC Consultation Statement)

BOOKS
Carson, D. A. (editor), *Biblical Interpretation and the Church,* (Exeter: Paternoster, 1984) (Eugene, Or: Wipf and Stock, 2002)
Carson, D. A. (editor), *Right with God: Justification in the Bible and the World* (Carlisle/Grand Rapids: Paternoster/Baker, 1992) (Eugene, Or: Wipf and Stock, 2002)

Carson, D. A. (editor), *Teach us to Pray: Prayer in the Bible and the World* (Exeter/Grand Rapids: Paternoster/Baker, 1990) (Eugene, Or: Wipf and Stock, 2002)

Carson, D. A. (editor), *The Church in the Bible and the World* (Exeter/Grand Rapids: Paternoster/Baker, 1987/1988) (Eugene, Or: Wipf and Stock, 2002)

Carson, D. A. (editor), *Worship: Adoration and Action* (Carlisle/Grand Rapids: Paternoster/Baker, 1993) (Eugene, Or: Wipf and Stock, 2002)

Cook, Matthew (Ed., et al), *Local Theology for the Global Church: Principles for an Evangelical Approach to Contextualization* (Los Angeles, Ca: William Carey, 2010)

Dowsett, Rose (editor), *Global Mission: Reflections and Case Studies in Contextualization for the Whole Church* (Pasadena, Calif.: William Carey Library, 2011).

Eber, Jochen (editor), *Hope does not Disappoint: Studies in Eschatology – essays from different contexts* (Bangalore/Bonn: TBT/Bonnermany by Verlag fuer Kultur und Wissenschaft, 2001)

Gnanakan, Ken, *Responsible Stewardship of God's Creation* (Bangalore: WEA Theological Commission/Theological Book Trust, 2004)

Holmes, Lionel J., *Church and Nationhood* (New Delhi: WEF Theological Commission, 1978). Papers originally presented at a Theological Commission consultation in Basel, September 1976

Nicholls, Bruce J. (editor), *Defending and Confirming the Gospel* (New Delhi: WEF Theological Commission, 1975). Papers and reports from the 1st Consultation held at the London Bible College, 8-12 Sept. 1975

Nicholls, Bruce J. (editor), *In Word and Deed: Evangelism and Social Responsibility* Grand Rapids, Eerdmans, 1986) (with Lausanne Committee on World Evangelisation). Papers presented at the Consultation on the Relationship between Evangelism and Social Responsibility, Reformed Bible College, Grand Rapids, Mich., June 16-23, 1982

Nicholls, Bruce J. (editor), *The Church: God's Agent for Change* (Exeter: Paternoster, 1986) published on behalf of the World Evangelical Fellowship. Selected papers from Wheaton '83, a conference convened by World Evangelical Fellowship at Wheaton College, Wheaton, Illinois, June 20-July 1, 1983

Nicholls, Bruce J. (editor), *The Unique Christ in our Pluralist World* (Carlisle/Grand Rapids: Paternoster/Baker, 1994). Published on behalf of the WEF Theological Commission. Papers originally presented at Manila, June 16-20, 1992

Nicholls, Bruce J. and Beulah Wood (editors), *Sharing Good News with the Poor* (Carlisle/Grand Rapids: Paternoster Press/Baker, 1996)

Nicholls, Bruce J. and Bong Rin Ro (editors), *Beyond Canberra: Evangelical responses to contemporary ecumenical issues* (Oxford: Regnum Books/Lynx Communications, 1993)

Parker David (ed.), *Jesus, Salvation and the Jewish People: Statement and Papers from Consultation on Jewish Evangelism* (Milton Keynes: Paternoster, 2011)

Parker, David, *'Discerning the Obedience of Faith' A Short History of the World Evangelical Alliance Theological Commission* (Bangalore: WEA Theological Commission/Theological Book Trust, 2005), updated edition 2014, World Theology Series No 3 (Bonn: Culture and Science Publishing, 2014)

Samuel, Vinay and Christopher Sugden (editors), *The Church in Response to Human Need* (Grand Rapids/Oxford: Eerdmans/Regnum Books, 1987 (Monrovia: MARC, 1983). Selected papers from Wheaton '83, a conference convened by the World Evangelical Fellowship at Wheaton College, Wheaton, Ill., June 20 – July 1, 1983

Sauer, Christof (editor), *Bad Urach Statement: Towards an evangelical theology of suffering, persecution and martyrdom for the global church in mission* (WEA Global Issues, 9) (Bonn: Culture and Science Publishing, 2012)

Sauer, Christof and Richard Howell (editors), *Suffering, Persecution and Martyrdom – Theological reflections*, (Religious Freedom Series, 2), (Kempton Park: AcadSA Publishing / Bonn: VKW, 2010)

Schirrmacher, Thomas (editor), *William Carey: Theologian – Linguist – Social Reformer* (World of Theology Series, Vol 4) (Bonn, Culture and Science Publishing, 2013)

Schirrmacher, Thomas, *Advocate of Love – Martin Bucer as Theologian and Pastor: Achieving Unity Through Listening to the Scriptures and Each Other* (World of Theology Series, Vol 5) (Bonn, Culture and Science Publishing, 2013)

Schirrmacher, Thomas, *Culture of Shame / Culture of Guilt* (World of Theology Series Vol 6) (Bonn, Culture and Science Publishing, 2013)

Schirrmacher, Thomas, *Racism* (WEA Global Issues Series, 8).(Bonn: Culture and Science Publishing: 2008)

Schirrmacher, Thomas, *The Koran and the Bible* (World of Theology Series, Vol 7) (Bonn, Culture and Science Publishing, 2013)

Schrotenboer, Paul (editor), *An Evangelical Response to 'Baptism, Eucharist and Ministry'* (Carlisle: Paternoster, 1992)

Schrotenboer, Paul G. (ed.), *Roman Catholicism: A Contemporary Evangelical Perspective* (Grand Rapids: Baker, 1988).

Sider, Ronald J., (editor), *Evangelicals and Development: Towards A Theology of Social Change* (Contemporary Issues In Social Ethics Vol 2) (Exeter: Paternoster, 1981. World Evangelical Fellowship Unit on Ethics and Society Consultation on the Theology of Development, 1980, High Leigh Conference Centre)

Sider, Ronald J., (editor), *Lifestyle in the Eighties: an Evangelical Commitment to Simple Lifestyle* (Contemporary Issues In Social Ethics Vol 1) (Exeter: Paternoster, 1982) Papers from the International Consultation on Simple Lifestyle, March 17-21, 1980, at High Leigh Conference Centre sponsored by the LCWE Theology and Education Group and the WEF TC Unit on Ethics and Society

Stott, J.R.W., *Evangelism and Social Responsibility: an Evangelical Commitment* (Exeter: Paternoster, 1982) WEF and LCWE. Papers presented at the Consultation on the Relationship between Evangelism and Social Responsibility, held at the Reformed Bible College, Grand Rapids, Mich., June 16-23, 1982

Taylor, William D, Antonia van der Meer and Reg Reimer (editors), *Sorrow & Blood: Christian Mission in Contexts of Suffering, Persecution, and Martyrdom* (Pasadena, Calif.: William Carey Library, 2013)

Wells, David F., *God the Evangelist: how the Holy Spirit works to bring men and women to faith* (Grand Rapids/Exeter: Eerdmans/Paternoster, 1987). A report of the Consultation on the Work of the Holy Spirit and Evangelization, 1985, Oslo, Norway

Wells, David F., *Turning to God: biblical conversion in the modern world* (Exeter/Grand Rapids: Paternoster/Baker, 1989). A report of the Consultation on Conversion, Hong Kong 4-8 January, 1988

Photos

Dr Bruce and Mrs Kathleen Nicholls,
Executive Director 1969-1986

Dr Sunand Sumithra,
Executive Director 1986-1989

Dr Bong Rin Ro,
Executive Director 1989-1996

Dr James Stamoolis,
Executive Director 1998-2001

Dr David Parker,
Administrator 1995-1996, 2003-2007;
Executive Director 2007-2009

Dr Rosalee Velloso Ewell,
Executive Director 2010-

Dr Byang Kato,
Chairman 1974-1975

Dr Arthur Climenhaga,
Chairman 1975-1980

Bishop David Gitari,
Chairman 1980-1986

Dr Peter Kusmic,
Chairman 1986-1996

Dr Rolf Hille,
Executive Chairman 1996-1998, 2001-2003;
Chairman 2003-2008

Dr Justin Thacker,
Chairman 2008-2010

Dr Thomas Schirrmacher,
Chairman 2010-

Miss (Dr) Patricia Harrison,
Secretary for TEE 1977-1983

Dr Paul Bowers,
General Secretary ICAA 1980-1982
and Administrator ICETE.

Dr Roger Kemp,
General Secretary ICAA 1989-1997

Dr George Vandervelde,
Convenor, Ecumenical Issues Task Force

Dr Ken Gnanakan,
Vice-chairman

Dr 'Jun' Vencer (International Director, WEF, 1992-2001)
Dr David Howard (International Director, WEF, 1982-1992)
Mr John E Langlois (TC Administrator 1969-1984 and General Treasurer, WEF)

Dr Rolf Hille and Dr Ken Gnanakan launching
'Responsible Stewardship of God's Creation' in Bangkok, October 2004

Dr James Nkansah-Obrempong
Vice-Chairman 2008-

Dr Brian Edgar
Executive Member

Dr David Hilborn
Executive Member

Dr Thomas C. Oden
Executive Member

Dr Claus Schwambach
Executive Member

Second TC Consultation, September 1976, on 'Church and Nationhood'
at St Chrischona, near Basel, Switzerland

Consultation on the Relationship between Evangelism and Social Responsibility
(CRESR), 16-23 June, 1982 at Grand Rapids, Michigan, USA

TC Consultation, April 9-14, 1996 on 'Faith and Hope for the Future'
at London Bible College, UK

TC Consultation, 27 June-2 July, 1986 on
'Christ our Liberator and Redeemer' at Singapore

Consultation on the Christian Gospel and Jewish People,
April 1989, at Willowbank, Bermuda

Ecumenical Issues Study Unit meeting at Deerfield, Ill., USA, June 1989

TC Consultation, June 18-22, 1990 on 'Theological Issues of the 90s' at Wheaton College, Ill, USA

TC Meeting, Bangkok, September 2004

Lausanne Theological Working Group Kenya 2007

Dr Thomas Schirrmacher in discussion after presenting WEA's view on Islam to an audience of WCC and Vatican in Geneva October 2008

Dr Rosalee Velloso Ewell at a conference at Bangalore
on the ethics of Christian mission, March 2012

Dr Rene Padilla and Dr David Parker
meet in Buenos Aries, Argentina, April 2008

Study Unit on Jewish evangelism meeting in Berlin, August 2008

Study Unit on Contextualisation meeting in Wycliffe Hall, Oxford August 2008

Joint TC Lausanne Theology Working Group consultation
at Limuru, Kenya, February 2007

TC and Korea Evangelical Theological Society Joint Consultation,
Seoul Korea, Sept-Oct 2005

TC Meeting in Philadelphia, July-August 2007

TC Consultation at Westminster Theological Seminary, Philadelphia, August 2007

Dr Thomas Schirrmacher given a plenary on behalf of the TC in the General Assembly of the World Council of Churches, Busan, Korea, 2013

TC Meeting and Consultation, Bangkok, October 2008

Dr C Schwambach and Dr J Thacker (on left) at TC Consultation,
Sao Paulo, Brazil, July 2009

Lausanne, ICETE, and TC of WEA joining for a conference of presidents of
theological seminaries from all continents in São Paulo 2014
(Dr. T. Schirrmacher sitting in the middle of the second row)

Index

Accreditation of theological education, 17, 20, 39
ACTS Institute, 41
AD 2000 Movement, 57, 62, 68
Adeyemo, Tokunboh, 27
Allan, John, 38, 51
AlphaGraphics Printing Services, 113, 125
Andersen, Neville, 16
Arana, Pedro, 53, 58, 109
Ashland Theological Seminary, 35
Asia Graduate School of Theology (AGST), 51, 55
Asia Theological Association (ATA), 15, 51, 52, 53, 55, 59, 91, 125
Asian Centre for Theological Studies (ACTS), 55
Asia-South Pacific Congress on Evangelism, 15
Association of Evangelicals of Africa and Madagascar (AEAM), 17, 31
Athyal, Saphir, 15
Au Sable, Institute of Environmental Studies, 57, 63
Australian Evangelical Alliance, 107
Authentic Media, 114
Baker Book House, 56
Bediako, Kwame, 60
Bennett, John 54
Berlin Statement on Jewish Evangelism, 112
Betz, Ulrich, 24
Beyerhaus, Peter, 16
Biblical library fund, 38

Billy Graham Centre Archives, 115
Blocher, Henri, 88
Bockmuehl, Klaus, 16, 24
Bowers, Paul, 20, 26, 30
Brattle, Liz 17
Bribery, 72
By-laws, TC, 46, 102
Cape Town 2010, 121
Caribbean Evangelical Association, 84
Carson, Donald A, 24, 27, 34, 41, 51, 53, 56, 57, 60
CD Rom, 84, 86, 91, 95, 98, 113, 125
Chao, Jonathan, 27, 43
China Church Research Centre, 43
China Ministries International, 43
Chow, Wilson, 95
Church and Nationhood Consultation 1976, 19
Clark, Dennis, 13
Climenhaga, Arthur, 16, 17
Code of Conduct: Christian witness in a multi-religious world, 123
Commission on women's concerns (CWC), 87, 88
Conference of itinerant evangelists, Amsterdam 2000, 84, 86
Consultation on the Relationship between Evangelism and Social Responsibility (CRESR) 1982, 22, 27
Contemporary Evangelical Perspectives on Roman Catholicism Report, 62
Contextual exegesis, 110, 112
Conversion, 43

Cook, Guillermo, 42
Cook, Matthew, 104, 105, 114
Daidanso, Rene, 34, 63
Dainton, Martin, 14
Early African Christianity, 104, 110, 112
East European Accreditation Association, 70
Eastern Europe, 57f
Eber, Jochen, 84, 99
Ecumenical Issues Task Force, 41, 53, 59, 62, 68, 71, 82, 97
Ecumenical Movement, 19
Edgar, Brian, 81, 94, 101, 107, 108, 111
Edmonds, Gary, 92, 94, 96, 97, 98, 101
Environment stewardship study project, 96, 98
Escobar, Samuel, 60
European Evangelical Alliance, 13
Evangelical Association for Theological Education in Latin America (AETAL), 58, 109
Evangelical Leadership Development Fund, 69
Evangelical Literature Trust, 26
Evangelical Lutheran Church in Wuerttemberg (ELCW), 47, 76, 93
Evangelical Review of Theology, ERT 25, 27, 34, 37, 52, 56, 59, 62, 70, 72, 76, 75, 80, 81, 85, 94, 110, 113, 116, 119, 124
Evangelical-Orthodox talks, 124
Evangelization, 62
Ewell, Rosalee Velloso, 122, 123f
Expository Preaching, 62
Faith and Church Study Unit, 41, 24, 56
Fellowship of European Evangelical Theologians (FEET), 44, 91, 93, 102
Financial support, 83, 91, 108

Forum on World Evangelization Pattaya Thailand 2004, 94, 95, 96, 97, 99, 110
Fundamentalism 104
Gasque, Ward, 53, 58, 78, 79
Gbonigi, Emmanuel, 59, 63, 73
Gerig, Zenas, 16
German Evangelical Alliance, 76
Gibson, Dwight, 79, 83
Gitari, David, 20, 27, 31, 33, 34
Global Christian Forum, 108, 124
Global Consultation on World Evangelization (GCOWE II), 62, 70, 74
Global Financial Crisis, 113
Global Issues series, 125
Global Membership Scheme, 102, 110, 124
Gnanakan, Ken, 41, 54, 54, 62, 79, 80, 81, 83, 84, 89, 90, 91, 96, 97, 98, 101, 104, 105, 106, 107, 125
Gospel and Culture Conference, Bermuda 1978, 18
Grounds, Vernon, 44
Gundry-Volf, Judy, 79
Hall, Chris, 107, 108
Harper, Michael, 42
Harrison, Patricia, 14, 20, 30, 36, 38
Hart, Richard, 30
Hiestand, Galen, 66
Hilborn, David, 90, 92, 95, 96, 97, 101, 103, 105, 107
Hille, Rolf, 34, 38, 45, 46, 60, 63, 75, 79, 80, 83, 84, 86, 92, 94, 95, 104, 105, 106, 107, 109, 112, 117, 121, 125, 126
HIV/AIDS, 104
Holmes, Lionel, 17, 23
Howard, David, 13, 31, 37, 51, 53, 54, 57
Inspiration, theory of biblical, 13
Integral Mission, 103

Index

Interchurch Relief and Development Alliance (IRDA), 79
International Consultation on Simple Lifestyle, 20, 21
International Council for Evangelical Theological Education (ICETE; see also ICAA), 70, 77, 79, 86, 93, 95, 96, 98, 101, 103, 125 (see also ICAA)
International Council of Accrediting Agencies (ICAA; see also ICETE), 18, 20, 26, 28, 30, 31, 38, 39, 45, 47, 48, 57, 58, 59, 66, 69, 70, 75, 77
International Fellowship of Evangelical Mission Theologians (INFEMIT), 23, 43, 60, 61
Internet, email and electronic communication, 54, 80, 81, 83, 115, 124, 125
Jewish evangelism, 44, 56, 97, 103, 106, 110, 112
Jews for Jesus, 44, 54
Johnson, Thomas K, 125
Justice, Peace and Integrity of Creation Conference March 1990, 53
Kantzer, Kenneth, 44
Kato, Byang, 16, 17, 19
Kemp, Roger, 26, 48, 58, 59, 77, 79
Kim, Jae Sung, 96, 102, 107
Kirby, Gilbert, 14
Kirk, J. Andrew, 30
Koorong Books Pty Ltd, 114
Korea Evangelical Theological Society (KETS), 71, 96, 98, 102
Korean Centre for World Missions, 71
Kuzmic, Peter, 33, 34, 54, 56, 57, 59, 72, 73, 75
Landreth, Gordon, 16
Langham Trust scholarship fund, 26, 85
Langham Trust/Partnership, 55, 66, 69, 123

Langlois, John E, 14, 16, 25, 30
Lausanne Committee for World Evangelization (LCWE), 17, 18, 28, 44, 51, 57, 94, 123
Lausanne Covenant 1974, 21
Lausanne Theology Working Group (TWG), 18, 21, 22, 23, 28, 44, 55, 94, 97, 98, 103, 105f, 109, 114, 122
Lee, Tony, 59
Lewis, Gordon, 54
Lewis, Peter, 54, 62
Liberation Theology, 33
Library development fund, 25, 55
Lillback, Peter, 107
Logos Bible Software, 125
London Bible College (London School of Theology), 14, 16, 60, 74
Manifesto on the Renewal of Theological Education, 28, 97
Mansur, Rodriguez Carlos, 92
McCain, Danny, 104
McKenna, David, 54f
McKinney, Lois, 26
Mudditt, B. Howard, 21
Mudditt, Jeremy, 21, 38, 51, 113
Muir, David, 17
Murdoch, Paul, 81
Nairobi Graduate School of Theology, 104
National Association of Evangelicals, USA, 17, 65
National Evangelical Fellowships, 67
Nazir-Ali, Michael, 34, 41, 53, 59
New Delhi TC office, 17[1]
Nicholls, Bruce 13, 16, 20, 29, 31, 32, 33, 34, 35, 37, 48, 51, 52, 59, 61, 68, 72, 73, 76, 80, 81, 125
Nicholls, Kathleen, 32
Nkansah-Obrempong, James 104, 107, 111, 117, 121
Nunez, Emilio, 53, 109

Oden, Thomas 88, 94, 104, 112
Operation Mobilisation (OM), 56
Orthodox Church Task Force, 83
Orthodox Churches, 19
Outreach and Identity Series, 24, 30, 67
Overseas Council for Theological Education, 26, 54, 57, 62, 66, 69, 70, 71
Oxford Centre for Mission Studies, 23, 46, 61
Packer, James I, 44, 56, 84
Padilla, Rene, 33, 42, 60, 109
Palmer Seminary, 107
Parker, David, 70, 72, 73, 76, 81, 83, 84, 87, 91, 95, 97, 105, 106, 107, 109, 111, 115, 119, 124
Pastoral Counselling Institute, 54
Paternoster Press, 21, 24, 38, 45, 51, 56, 70, 72, 85, 113
Pederson, Per, 98, 101
Perez, Pablo, 20, 21, 29
Programming News, 14
Relief and Development agencies, 20
Research Information Bank, 17
Ro, Bong Rin, 15, 16, 51, 55, 57, 66, 67, 68, 69, 71, 72, 73, 79
Roldan, David, 111, 116
Roman Catholic Church, 19, 27, 33, 53f, 62, 68, 71, 72, 90, 91, 94, 96, 98, 101, 103, 106, 196, 110, 123, 125
Roman Catholicism, Task force, 21
Roman Catholic-WEA talks, 81, 85, 87, 92
Roxborogh, John, 70
Salinas, Daniel, 116
Samuel, Vinay, 21, 27, 42, 60
Saracco, Norberto, 117
Savage, Peter, 16
Schirrmacher, Thomas, 117, 119, 120, 121, 123, 124
Scholarship fund, 26, 27, 38, 55, 62, 67, 70, 71, 75

Schrotenboer, Paul 27, 32, 33, 34, 40, 41, 51, 53, 59, 62, 71, 72, 82
Schwambach, Claus 98, 107, 109, 116
Scott, Waldron, 60
Send the Light (STL), 56, 113
Seoul Declaration, 23
Seventh-Day Adventist Church 103
Sider, Ronald, 20, 21, 27, 42, 60, 107
Sine, Tom, 29
Son, Bong Ho, 42, 63, 68, 73
Sookhdeo, Patrick, 27, 29, 41
Spicer, Charles 57
St. Chrischona Seminary, Basel Switzerland, 19, 23
Stamoolis, James, 83, 84, 85, 87, 89, 90
Steuernagel, Valdir, 117
Stott, John R W, 16, 18, 22, 25, 26
Study Unit, Ecumenical Issues, 21
Study Unit, Ethics and Society Study Unit, 20, 27, 33, 43, 53, 57, 62, 63, 72
Study Unit, Pastoral Ministries, 54
Study Unit, Theological Education, 14, 38, 45, 48
Study Unit, Theological Education, 20, 46
Study Units and Task Forces, 18, 23, 27, 51, 53, 59, 66, 70, 80, 84
Sugden, Chris, 21, 42, 60, 62, 63
Sumithra, Sunand, 31, 32, 37, 36, 40, 44, 45, 47, 51, 52
Tan, David, 40
Tano, Rodrigo, 33, 55
Task Force - Eastern Europe Needs and Issues, 54, 59
Taylor, Clyde, 15
Teng, Philip, 16
Thacker, Justin, 107, 109, 111, 114, 115, 117, 119
The Basel Letter, 19

Index

Theological Assistance Program (TAP), 14, 15, 16, 51
Theological Commission (TC), 13, 16, 17, 46, 102
Theological Commission, difficulties, financial and structural, 85
Theological Commission, vision statement, 86f, 116
Theological Education by Extension (TEE), 14
Theological Education Today (TET), 14, 38
Theological Education, 35, 97
Theological educational development fund, 66
Theological News (TN), 14, 25, 37, 52, 72, 73, 81, 87, 94, 112, 115, 117, 120, 124
Theological Research and Communication Institute (TRACI), 17
Theological Resource Library – see CD-ROM
Theology of Evangelization, 59
Third World theologians, Conference, Seoul, Korea, 1982, 23
Tienou, Tite, 31, 32
Tinder, Donald, 89
Transformation, 27, 30, 33, 43, 46, 60, 61
Tunnicliffe, Geoff, 101, 103, 108, 111, 124, 125
Turaki, Yusufu, 104
Ullah, Frank Khair, 20
Union Biblical Seminary, Yeotmal India 13, 15, 31

Vandervelde, George, 34, 53, 82, 90, 97, 101, 105 106, 108
Vargas, Marcelo, 116
Vencer, Augustin (Jun), 65, 66, 69, 73, 83, 91
Wells, David, 28, 46
Westminster Theological Seminary 107
White, Paul S, 16
Willowbank Consultation, 44
Willowbank, 54
Wong, Kim Kong, 98
World Council of Churches (WCC), 19, 40, 53, 58, 62, 67, 103, 123, 124
World Directory of Theological Institutions, 68
World Evangelical Alliance, also known as World Evangelical Fellowship, 13, 31, 33, 21, 45, 51, 92, 97
World Evangelical Alliance, General Assembly 21, 30, 31, 33, 38, 61, 70, 72, 76, 80, 87, 88, 109, 110, 112
World Evangelical Alliance, name change, 92
World Evangelical Alliance, statement of faith, 95, 101, 103
World of Theology Series, 125
World Vision, 104
Wright, Christopher J H, 103, 105, 110, 120, 123, 125
Youngblood, Robert, 26, 27, 30, 31, 38, 40, 46, 47
Yu, Carver, 98, 103, 121, 123
Zaretsky, Tuvya, 44, 54

World Evangelical Alliance

World Evangelical Alliance is a global ministry working with local churches around the world to join in common concern to live and proclaim the Good News of Jesus in their communities. WEA is a network of churches in 129 nations that have each formed an evangelical alliance and over 100 international organizations joining together to give a worldwide identity, voice and platform to more than 600 million evangelical Christians. Seeking holiness, justice and renewal at every level of society – individual, family, community and culture, God is glorified and the nations of the earth are forever transformed.

Christians from ten countries met in London in 1846 for the purpose of launching, in their own words, "a new thing in church history, a definite organization for the expression of unity amongst Christian individuals belonging to different churches." This was the beginning of a vision that was fulfilled in 1951 when believers from 21 countries officially formed the World Evangelical Fellowship. Today, 150 years after the London gathering, WEA is a dynamic global structure for unity and action that embraces 600 million evangelicals in 129 countries. It is a unity based on the historic Christian faith expressed in the evangelical tradition. And it looks to the future with vision to accomplish God's purposes in discipling the nations for Jesus Christ.

Commissions:

- Theology
- Missions
- Religious Liberty
- Women's Concerns
- Youth
- Information Technology

Initiatives and Activities

- Ambassador for Human Rights
- Ambassador for Refugees
- Creation Care Task Force
- Global Generosity Network
- International Institute for Religious Freedom
- International Institute for Islamic Studies
- Leadership Institute
- Micah Challenge
- Global Human Trafficking Task Force
- Peace and Reconciliation Initiative
- UN-Team

Church Street Station
P.O. Box 3402
New York, NY 10008-3402
Phone +[1] 212 233 3046
Fax +[1] 646-957-9218
www.worldea.org

Giving Hands

GIVING HANDS GERMANY (GH) was established in 1995 and is officially recognized as a nonprofit foreign aid organization. It is an international operating charity that – up to now – has been supporting projects in about 40 countries on four continents. In particular we care for orphans and street children. Our major focus is on Africa and Central America. GIVING HANDS always mainly provides assistance for self-help and furthers human rights thinking.

The charity itself is not bound to any church, but on the spot we are co-operating with churches of all denominations. Naturally we also cooperate with other charities as well as governmental organizations to provide assistance as effective as possible under the given circumstances.

The work of GIVING HANDS GERMANY is controlled by a supervisory board. Members of this board are Manfred Feldmann, Colonel V. Doner and Kathleen McCall. Dr. Christine Schirrmacher is registered as legal manager of GIVING HANDS at the local district court. The local office and work of the charity are coordinated by Rev. Horst J. Kreie as executive manager. Dr. theol. Thomas Schirrmacher serves as a special consultant for all projects.

Thanks to our international contacts companies and organizations from many countries time and again provide containers with gifts in kind which we send to the different destinations where these goods help to satisfy elementary needs. This statutory purpose is put into practice by granting nutrition, clothing, education, construction and maintenance of training centers at home and abroad, construction of wells and operation of water treatment systems, guidance for self-help and transportation of goods and gifts to areas and countries where needy people live.

GIVING HANDS has a publishing arm under the leadership of Titus Vogt, that publishes human rights and other books in English, Spanish, Swahili and other languages.

These aims are aspired to the glory of the Lord according to the basic Christian principles put down in the Holy Bible.

Baumschulallee 3a • D-53115 Bonn • Germany
Phone: +49 / 228 / 695531 • Fax +49 / 228 / 695532
www.gebende-haende.de • info@gebende-haende.de

Martin Bucer Seminary

Faithful to biblical truth
Cooperating with the Evangelical Alliance
Reformed

Solid training for the Kingdom of God
- Alternative theological education
- Study while serving a church or working another job
- Enables students to remain in their own churches
- Encourages independent thinking
- Learning from the growth of the universal church.

Academic
- For the Bachelor's degree: 180 Bologna-Credits
- For the Master's degree: 120 additional Credits
- Both old and new teaching methods: All day seminars, independent study, term papers, etc.

Our Orientation:
- Complete trust in the reliability of the Bible
- Building on reformation theology
- Based on the confession of the German Evangelical Alliance
- Open for innovations in the Kingdom of God

Our Emphasis:
- The Bible
- Ethics and Basic Theology
- Missions
- The Church

Our Style:
- Innovative
- Relevant to society
- International
- Research oriented
- Interdisciplinary

Structure
- 15 study centers in 7 countries with local partners
- 5 research institutes
- President: Prof. Dr. Thomas Schirrmacher
  Vice President: Prof. Dr. Thomas K. Johnson
- Deans: Thomas Kinker, Th.D.;
  Titus Vogt, lic. theol., Carsten Friedrich, M.Th.

Missions through research
- Institute for Religious Freedom
- Institute for Islamic Studies
- Institute for Life and Family Studies
- Institute for Crisis, Dying, and Grief Counseling
- Institute for Pastoral Care

www.bucer.eu • info@bucer.eu
Berlin I Bielefeld I Bonn I Chemnitz I Hamburg I Munich I Pforzheim
Innsbruck I Istanbul I Izmir I Linz I Prague I São Paulo I Tirana I Zurich

www.ingramcontent.com/pod-product-compliance
Lightning Source LLC
Chambersburg PA
CBHW050824160426
43192CB00010B/1881